WORCESTER CATHEDRAL

WORCESTER CATHEDRAL
A SHORT HISTORY

by
Philip Barker MA, FSA, HonMIFA
&
Christopher Romain BA, B. Arch., RIBA, AABC, FRSA
&
Christopher Guy BA, MIFA

Logaston Press
in association with
Chris Romain Architecture

LOGASTON PRESS
Little Logaston, Woonton, Almeley
Herefordshire HR3 6QH

CHRIS ROMAIN ARCHITECTURE
45 Salisbury Road,
Fordingbridge, Hampshire SP6 1EH

First published by Logaston Press 2007
Copyright © Chris Romain 2007

ISBN 978 1904396 81 9

Set in Times New Roman by Logaston Press
and printed in Great Britain by
Bell & Bain Ltd, Glasgow

Contents

Philip Barker, 1920-2001, to whom this book is dedicated

Acknowledgements

Thanks are due to all the following for their indispensable help in the production of this book: The Chapter of Worcester and Mr Les West, the Steward and Chapter Clerk; the much missed late Canon Iain Mackenzie and Dr David Morrison, cathedral librarian; previous cathedral architects Kenneth Wiltshire and the late Bernard Ashwell. I am also grateful to my wife, Ann, for revising the text.

The photographs are by the authors unless otherwise attributed.

Readers may also be interested in following the developing study of the architecture and archaeology of the cathedral may wish to purchase copies of the report of the Annual Symposia, published by the Chapter of Worcester Cathedral, Chapter office, 10A College green, Worcester WR1 2LH.

Introduction

The first edition of this short history by Philip Barker was published in 1994. This is the third edition, produced to meet continuing demand for a readable, concise history of this fascinating building.

It is now six years since Philip's death, but his gift of inspiring others to observe and analyse the evidence available, remains.

In this edition, I am joined by Chris Guy, the Cathedral Archaeologist, who has contributed so much to this 'all colour' version.

Chris Romain   Worcester 2007

Preface

There is no short, easily accessible account of the architectural development of Worcester Cathedral. This book attempts to fill that gap, but in order to make it concise and readable, it has been necessary to simplify drastically a large and complex building, to resist dwelling on detailed discussion, and sometimes to side-step controversial questions of date or influence.

Worcester's site has been continuously occupied since at least late prehistoric times, and archaeology, topography and documentary history are beginning to make clear the outlines of the development of the city from the earliest times to the present day. Nevertheless, the architectural evolution of Worcester's principal church is known only from the Norman Conquest onwards — the histories of the churches which preceded St Wulfstan's new church of 1084 are known only in barest outline, and their architectural development — even their sites — are quite unknown.

Since it is unlikely that documents relating to the pre-Norman churches remain to be discovered, further research into the early churches' sites and structures will principally be archaeological, using mainly geophysical survey and excavation. Geophysical surveys, being non-destructive, must be the first option, though they have limitations which are not yet understood. Meanwhile every opportunity to observe and record holes dug, for whatever cause, in and around the cathedral must be taken in the hope that fragments of information will accumulate, like pieces of a jigsaw, to build a fuller picture of the past than we have today. Although we are near the end of a massive and expensive programme of restoration, there are no funds or time for research excavation on the scale required to solve some of the more intractable problems of the early churches and their surrounding monastic buildings, but economic and academic climates may change, and research excavations become possible in the comparatively near future. Meanwhile, the only excavations carried out are those demanded by the restoration programme or other emergencies.

It is difficult to write about a great building with a long history of additions, alterations and repairs, without using some technicalities. While these have been kept to a minimum, readers not familiar with architectural terms will find explanatory diagrams and a glossary at the end of the book.

This book attempts to distil the work of many scholars, architectural historians and archaeologists. In order to avoid the mass of references which would be necessary to justify every statement or opinion, these also are kept to a minimum, but lists of books containing supporting evidence and others for further reading will also be found at the end of the book.

1. THE SITE OF THE CATHEDRAL

Fig.1 Topographical map of the site of Worcester showing the strategic position of the defended core of the city at the southern tip of a ridge of sand and gravel close to a crossing point of the Severn. (Reproduced from Barker, 1970)

Worcester is situated on the southern tip of a long ridge of sand and gravel which forms one of the terraces of the Severn laid down in post-glacial times on the edge of the river's flood plain. The suburb of St John's stands on the opposite terrace. The city occupies a promontory bounded by the Severn on the west and the once marshy valley of the Frog Brook on the east. The river was tidal until the construction of Diglis Weir in the 19th century, and the crossing point here would have been fordable at least twice a day, and more often when the river was low. The combination of a naturally defended site and the crossing of a major river made it an obvious choice for settlement, and Worcester's first defences probably date from the late Iron Age, that is, the last few centuries before Christ.

Fig. 2 The development of Worcester from late Roman times up till the early 13th century, showing the positions of the early churches and the cathedral in relation to the defences.

2.   FROM ROMAN *VERTIS* TO NORMAN *WIRECESTRE*

Roman Worcester, whose name may have been Vertis, though this is not certain, occupied the same defended area as the Iron Age site, and a suburb, at first residential though later given over to iron-smelting, developed to the north. In the later Roman period the town's defences were massively enlarged on the same alignment and by this time a stone bridge may have been built a little upstream from the site of the present bridge.

Although the years between the early 5th and the late 9th centuries are obscure, there is now convincing evidence of continuity of occupation of Worcester from Roman times through to the building of the Anglo-Saxon burh c.880-890. This evidence derives in part from archaeology, but more from the study of the topography and the ecclesiastical history of the city.

It has been suggested that Worcester's strategic importance as a defended bridge-head on the Severn may have increased in the early post-Roman period (Bassett, 1989, 247) and that the large well-defined territory which was apparently subject to Worcester's British rulers became the parish of a church which stood in the defended enclosure. This was St Helen's. Bassett continues 'there may well be nothing Roman about St Helen's, Worcester, or about the territory around the town which became its parish, but there can be no doubt that when the first Anglo-Saxon bishop of the Hwicce arrived there, he came to a place which was already an important Christian centre; nor that the minster founded for him was meant to take over (at least at local level) from an established British church — probably a see—serving a wide rural hinterland'

(*op. cit.* 248). Two other early churches lay within the northern defences of the town — St Margaret's (now lost) and St Alban's (Baker, *et al.* 1992).

It is not clear why St Helen's, St Alban's and St Margaret's churches were all sited within the northern edge of the enclosure (fig. 2), but it has been reasonably suggested that this was because the rest of the enclosure was already occupied by buildings, perhaps dating from Roman times and still in use. While no Roman stone buildings are known from within the defended circuit, small excavations have shown that below the medieval and Anglo-Saxon occupation levels lies deep building debris including masses of roof tiles, suggesting that the Roman buildings here were of timber. Excavation in other Roman towns, for example Wroxeter in Shropshire, has shown that major buildings could be constructed of timber, so it may be that the centre of the enclosure contained Roman public buildings, or perhaps a complex of domestic buildings, all of timber. These may still have been in use in the late and sub-Roman periods, that is, the 4th to the 6th centuries AD. Scattered patches of a Roman slag and pebble surface found beneath the chapter house in 2003 may be the remains of a yard as they were over too wide an area to have been part of a road. From the cathedral itself the evidence for continuity of Christian worship from Roman times is significant though not conclusive. In 1970 two east-west burials of young men were found immediately under the floor of the refectory undercroft (front end paper, Z). Calibrated radio-carbon dates of two samples from one skeleton using two standard deviations give ranges of AD 416-811 (or 852) for one sample, (A), and AD 449-886 for the other, (B). The see was founded in AD 680. The date for sample A therefore lies between 264 years before the foundation of the see and 172 years after it. Similarly the date for sample B lies between 231 years before the foundation of the see and 206 years after it. The balance of these dates lies slightly before rather than after 680. There is, however, another factor which tilts the burial dates back towards Roman times. This is the discovery, under the neck of one of the bodies, of a tiny fragment of very fine gold braid dated by Elizabeth Crowfoot, who examined it, to either the late Roman or the late Saxon period. As the calibrated radio-carbon dates above include the late Roman but not the late Saxon period, the balance of probability suggests that the actual dates may be before (perhaps well before) 680, the date

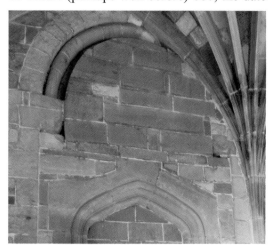

Fig. 3 Part of the west wall of the cloister showing the large semi-circular arched opening cut into it. This opening has the same characteristics as Wulfstan's church — a roll moulding and simple cushion capitals. The wall into which it is cut is therefore presumed to be Anglo-Saxon. The four-centred arched doorway below is of the 14th century.

of the foundation of the see. (Barker *et al.*, 1974 and Bassett, 1989)

The origins of the Anglo-Saxon tribe of the Hwicce, which occupied the area which eventually became the diocese of Worcester, are obscure, but they were in existence as a political unit by the early 7th century (Wilson, M. in Barker *et al.*, 1970). In the reorganisation of the English church, Archbishop Theodore established a see at Worcester and its first Bishop, Bosel, took office in 680.

By that time, the majority of any late Roman buildings may have fallen into disuse (the two burials under the refectory suggest that part at least of the central area had become a cemetery) leaving an open space in which Bosel could build the first cathedral, dedicated to St Peter. We have no idea what this cathedral was like, nor even whether it was built of timber or stone, though as it was 'still standing' in 991, and its presbytery was enlarged in stone after *c.*1040-41, it seems likely that it was a stone building from the first.

We do not know precisely where it was, though presumably it was within the present precinct. It has been suggested that it may have lain to the south, in the area of College Green, and been incorporated after the Conquest into the bailey of the Norman castle, though if this were so, it is remarkable that such a loss to the monastery is not mentioned when the loss of part of the monks' cemetery to the castle bailey is recorded and deplored. It is more likely that it lay beneath the present cathedral, particularly as a lay cemetery of Anglo-Saxon date lies under the chapter house.

In 961 Oswald became bishop and, as one of the leading figures in the monastic reform movement, replaced the secular priests who had served the cathedral by a more formally organised monastic community. To house the new community he built a cathedral dedicated to St Mary. Presumably this church was begun some time in the 960s and according to a note attached to a charter of 983, the cathedral of St Mary was completed in that year. Another charter tells us that the church of St Peter was still standing in 991, and that the Bishop's throne was still housed in the old building.

Two writers, Hemming in the 11th century and William of Malmesbury in the 12th century, believed that St Mary's had been built in the cemetery of St Peter's. Hemming described Oswald, before the completion of his new church, preaching to large crowds, standing on the stone tomb of an 8th-century nobleman and his wife. The tomb stood till the 1040s, when it was demolished to provide building material for the enlargement of St Peter's, mentioned above. St Peter's thus remained in use until at least the mid-11th century — after that nothing more is heard of it. St Mary's had a bell tower added to it in the 1050s by Wulfstan, who was then prior.

The Norman castle at Worcester, a timber castle of motte and bailey type, was in existence within three years of the Conquest, in 1069, when Urse d'Abitot was appointed constable. He constructed an outer bailey 'digging a ditch across the monks' burial ground'. A writer of the 18th century says 'The precincts of the church were very strait or scant as it were "pent up" between the south side of the church and the north side of the castle'. However, since the monks recovered their burial ground in 1217 it is not clear how the writer knew this in the 18th century.

In 1084, 15 years after the building of the castle, Wulfstan began an entirely new and, by comparison, huge church, large parts of which still stand today, incorporated into the fabric of the present cathedral.

Some possible pre-Norman Walls

The west wall of the cloister, part of which was the party wall with the dormitory beyond, has, since the 19th century, been described as Anglo-Saxon, because of the large early Norman opening (now blocked) which has been cut into it (fig. 3). Another wall, west of the dormitory, and forming the east wall of the undercroft between the dormitory and the river, is also said to be Anglo-Saxon, because it is made of large, heavily-weathered stones, against which the 12th-century vaulting of the undercroft has been built. Clearly it had been an exterior wall for a long time before the vaulting was added to it. (*Worcs. Cath. Notes etc. 1909-1914*)

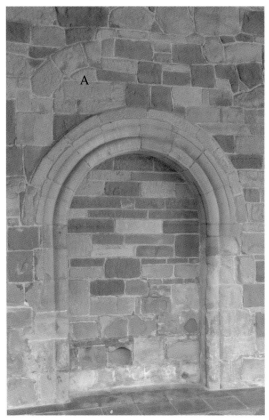

Fig. 4 A detail of the west wall of the cloister showing a blocked Norman door with, at A, a fragment of an earlier window. The masonry to the right of the blocked door may be pre-Norman. The masonry blocking the Norman door appears to have been built in imitation of the pre-Norman masonry. All the cloister walls deserve very careful analysis.

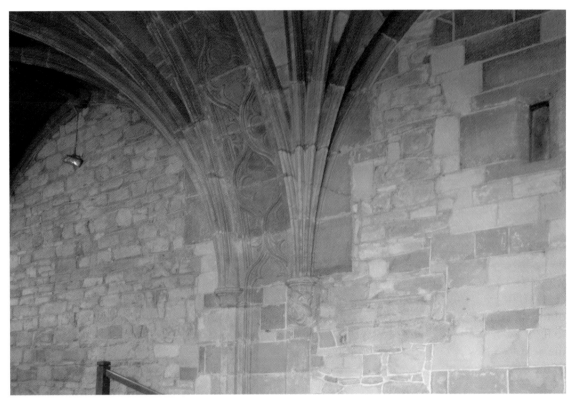

Fig. 5 The wall of the eastern cloister walk between the eastern slype and the nave of the church. The coursed rubble wall appears to be earlier than the ashlar wall to the right, which is keyed into it. Since the ashlar wall is part of the 1084+ stair turret in the corner of the south transept, it follows that the rubble wall is earlier and therefore may be Anglo-Saxon. The attached shafts and springers of the cloister vault are, of course, later inserts of the 14th century.

There is a very similar length of wall at the extreme west end of the refectory undercroft, which, although now an internal wall, seems to have been weathered in the same way, and therefore appears also to have been external at some time.

There are two other stretches of wall in the cloister which appear to be earlier than the Norman walls which butt against them. One is the west wall of the transept between the Prior's Door and the 11th-century turret in the corner of the transept which appears to have been keyed into the coursed rubble of the transept wall (fig. 5). The other is in the cloister south wall, where part of the wall, which is of course the north wall of the refectory, is also

of coursed rubble, quite different from the rest of the wall and its buttresses which are of large rectangular blocks of red sandstone. Examination of the junction of the rubble wall where it meets the buttress to its east shows that the buttress is partly built against the wall and partly keyed into it. Clearly the buttress is later (fig. 6).

The common characteristics of these early rubble walls are the variety of stones used, the frequent use of diagonal joints or triangular stones and, at intervals of two or three courses, thinner courses not unlike the tile courses in much Roman masonry. The western face of the western wall of the cloister (fig. 7), now an exterior face but originally the interior wall of the east end of the dormitory, shows this characteristic clearly now it has been weathered, since the lias, which forms the narrow coursing on this side, stands proud of the rest of the wall, which is of softer Highley stone. It is interesting that, though the two sides of the same wall are built of different materials, the constructional techniques are similar.

The significance of these early stretches of wall is not obvious. If they really are pre-Conquest they are presumably remains from the Anglo-Saxon monastic buildings. It is curious that they are built into three sides of the present cloister and the most obvious explanation would be that the Anglo-Saxon cloister was the same size as the present one, which seems inherently unlikely. The three sections of the wall need not, of course, have belonged to the same building, and the misalignment of the refectory with the cathedral and the rest of the monastic buildings (see front endpaper) may derive from its re-use of the foundations of an earlier building, of which the stretch of rubble wall in the cloister and the stretch of apparently external wall in the undercroft are all that survive above ground.

Large sections of early wall within the cathedral are also built in somewhat similar techniques, for example, the west wall of the northern transept (fig. 9) contrasting with the adjoining stair turret.

The use of this somewhat similar walling in the early cathedral might be explained by the use of Anglo-Saxon masons to build lengths of wall in the manner to which they were accustomed, with Norman masons building alongside them in ashlar, for example, in the stair turrets.

The plain red sandstone walls in the north and south walks of the cloisters, with their simple square-section buttresses, appear at first sight to be Norman (a view endorsed by Pevsner, p.298). However, there are compelling arguments for believing them to be of the late 13th or early 14th centuries, although the section below the benching against the south wall of the nave could well be Norman. Indeed, Pevsner's plan of the cathedral (*ibid.*, p.296) shows these sections of wall as belonging to the 14th century. If so, the coursed rubble section of the cloister south walk may well be Norman rather than Anglo-Saxon.

Fig. 6 A detail of the south wall of the cloister, i.e. the north wall of the refectory, showing a buttress of massive squared ashlar with a similar wall to the left, and, to the right, a wall of roughly coursed rubble which runs behind the buttress which has been alternately keyed into it. The rubble wall is therefore earlier and possibly pre-Norman. The springing of the vault above is late-14th century and can be seen to have been inserted.

Fig. 7 The exterior of the west wall of the cloister, showing the blocked Perpendicular doorway into the dormitory, D, and the blocked rectangular windows, E, above the present, late, doorway into the garden. The wall, which has thin courses of lias alternating with Highley stone has, since the 19th century, been thought to be Anglo-Saxon. It is unique in the cathedral and in its construction, as is the cloister side of the same wall (fig. 4).

All this is pure speculation, of course, but there are problems here which cannot be easily explained, and the more one examines these walls the more intractable the problems become.

3.   St Wulfstan's Cathedral

St Wulfstan became bishop in 1062 and, surviving the Norman Conquest, remained so until his death in 1095. The two Anglo-Saxon cathedrals had been sacked by the Danes in the early 11th century and though we do not know the extent of the destruction it was certainly not total. When Wulfstan became bishop he found only 12 monks at the monastery and he increased this number to 50 and acquired estates to finance the enlarged establishment. The old minsters must by now have become inconvenient and it would clearly be more suitable to have one much larger church. However, political considerations may have played their part and Wulfstan could have been ordered by William to build a 'Norman' cathedral. According to the *Worcester Annals* work began in 1084 and by 1089 the new church was sufficiently far advanced for the monks to move into it. This must mean that within five years the crossing and the eastern bays of the nave, together with the presbytery and the crypt beneath, were completed. William of Malmesbury says that 'When the work of the main church, which he had begun from the foundations, had advanced to that stage of growth that now the monks might move into it, the old church which blesséd Oswald had built was ordered to be unroofed and destroyed.' This suggests, though it does not prove, that the old church lay in the area of the present nave or cloister.

It is significant that Wulfstan had a remarkably modern view of the destruction of ancient buildings, saying: 'We miserable people have destroyed the work of saints, pompously thinking we can do better: how much more eminent than us was St Oswald who built this church; how many holy men of religion have served God in it.'

In spite of this he pulled down Oswald's church.

We do not know when the rest of the church, that is, the western part of the nave, was completed, but presumably it was part of the building campaign which added the cloister and the monastic buildings, including the chapter house, in the early years of the 12th century. We know nothing, at present, about the Anglo-Saxon monastic buildings which these new buildings replaced.

Wulfstan's church was constructed in pale Cotswold limestone and in green Highley sandstone and was simple and massive, and there is ample evidence that it was largely white-washed both inside and out. A small fragment of the outside of the crypt was found in excavations in 1986-87 and shows that the masonry, though fine, was plastered, whitened and false-jointed, that is, had joints drawn on it in dark paint (fig. 8a). Areas of similar though later false jointing can be seen at the western end of the choir at triforium level (figs. 8b and 8c) — from the ground they are almost completely deceptive.

Apart from the crypt, enough fragments of Wulfstan's church remain to enable us to say with certainty that his church was as wide as the present church, the nave was as long, and the tower and the western transepts were the same area as those which replaced them. The front endpaper shows the positions of these surviving parts of the early Norman church and figs. 8-14 and 18-21 are photographs or drawings of most of them.

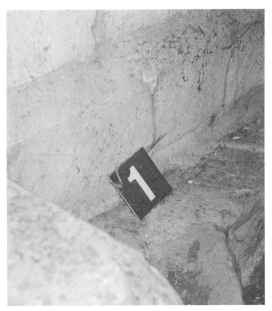

Fig. 8a Fragment of the exterior plinth of Wulfstan's church, revealed in the crypt excavations of 1986-7, showing the plastered and whitewashed wall with false-jointing.

Fig. 8b Part of the Norman choir arcade incorporated into the wall of the Early English choir arcade.

Fig. 8c Part of the Norman gallery arcade embedded above 8b in the Early English choir triforium. The massive half drum respond seen in fig. 16 lies on the other side of this wall.

Much of the apparent stonework here is false-jointing painted on plaster in an attempt to mask the junction of the Early English and Norman masonry, with the 14th-century tower pier just in the picture on the left. (Photograph by courtesy of Conway Library, Courtauld Institute of Art)

For example, fragments of evidence which prove that the first Norman church was as long as the present church are two column bases preserved on the outside of the west door, itself rebuilt in the late 12th century. These survivals show not only that the Norman church was the same length but that the doorway was the same width, as it has

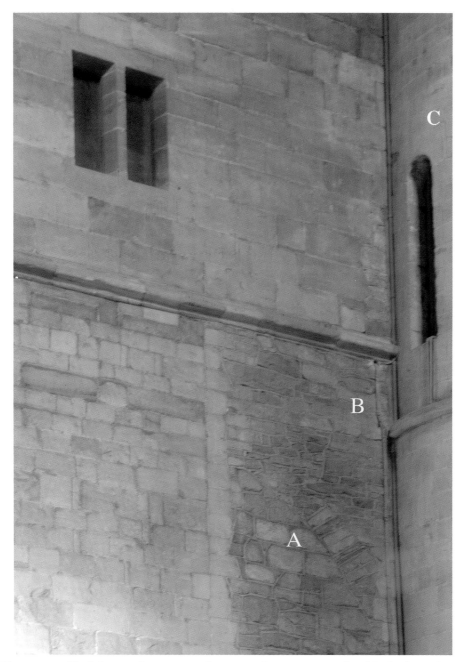

Fig. 9 The west wall of the north transept showing a large rectangular blocked window space, presumably of the 14th/15th century, which had been cut into the Norman wall which abuts the stair turret on the extreme right. The plain wall, which would have been plastered, is of coursed rubble construction unlike the turret which is of fine ashlar with banded masonry at the bottom. The possible significance of this difference is discussed on p.7. At A is the scar of the vault which held the gallery of Wulfstan's church whose floor was at the level of the string course at B. At C is a window converted from the door which led from the stair turret out on to the gallery.

Fig. 10 The north-east corner of the north-west transept showing fragments of earlier walling and, at D, the springing of an arch of the 11th-century gallery.

Fig. 11 A surviving attached shaft E of Wulfstan's church, (at D on front endpaper) contrasting with the 14th-century shafts F beyond.

Fig. 12 The north door of the cathedral showing the two attached shafts C, C with plain capitals and bases showing that the north door of Wulfstan's church was here and was the same size as the present door. The rest of the doorway and the porch date from 1386, though the whole front was taken down and rebuilt in the 19th-century restoration. There is documentary evidence (quoted in Felicitas Corrigan, The Nun, the Infidel and the Superman, *p.36) that there was a large porch over the 11th-century door, in which the cantors, four or five monks and boys, had stood to sing the Gloria Laus.*

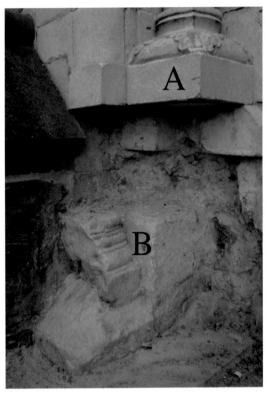

been shown to be in the north porch (figs. 12 and 13). Excavations within the north porch in 1996 to improve access revealed a chamfered step between the surviving shaft bases. However, unlike the present situation, it was a step up into the cathedral.

As a result of these fortunate survivals, we have been able to draw a conjectural reconstruction of Wulfstan's church (fig. 14) which, while perhaps not exact in all its details, must give a close impression of its scale and its massive simplicity — a great white building, by far the largest in Worcester, dominating the city. Its absence of external decoration contrasts sharply with that of the Gothic cathedral which replaced it — compare for instance, our reconstruction of Wulfstan's tower with the present 14th-century tower (fig. 75).

In addition to the fragments visible in the church, work in the north choir triforium in 1991 revealed an almost complete respond, massively semi-circular in section, with a capital which is clearly of Wulfstan's period (figs. 16 and 17). This was an unexpected discovery and shows that the gallery to which

Fig. 13 (Left) The northern base of the west door showing the 12th-century base, A, above the buried 11th-century base, B, revealed here by excavation.

Fig. 14 Reconstruction of Wulfstan's church by Peter Scholefield.

Fig. 15a and b. Capitals from the arch between the south transept and the former east transept chapel, now the John chapel. Their date is a matter for discussion but is between 1100 and 1120 and based on Anglo-Saxon models.

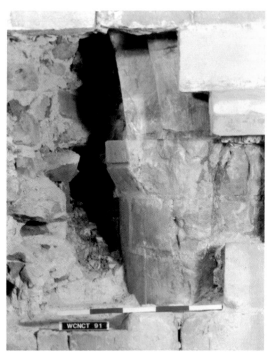

Fig. 16 The semi-circular respond or half-pier of the gallery of Wulfstan's church found embedded in the 13th-century wall of the triforium on the north side of the choir. The simple capital is similar to that of the central column of the chapter house. Short drum columns like this are found in the gallery at Gloucester. It is probable that the columns of the chancel of Wulfstan's church were also drum shaped, anticipating those of Gloucester, Hereford, Tewkesbury and Malvern.

Fig. 17 An axonometric reconstruction of the respond. (Drawing by Chris Guy)

it belonged must have been very like that surviving at Gloucester, though the Worcester gallery is some years earlier.

Internally, Wulfstan's church, though the same size, was very different from the present cathedral. Dr Richard Gem has shown that instead of a triforium at first storey level it had galleries which ran round the whole church (figs. 18 and 20). In fact, recent excavations near the tower piers have revealed massive square bases which supported vaults covering the whole areas of both transepts (fig. 21). In

effect, this first Norman church was of two storeys, the extra floor space used principally to house chapels and altars.

While there were massive columnar piers in both storeys of the chancel east of the crossing, the nave arcade was composed of compound piers, that is with groups of attached shafts, two of which can be seen in the second piers from the west end of the nave (fig. 19). In the excavations of the tower piers, the massive foundations of Wulfstan's time were found to be bluntly cross-shaped so it is probable that the piers of the nave were cross-shaped also. The galleries of the nave had double openings above the nave arches and while the chancel was very probably barrel vaulted, the nave almost certainly had a wooden roof.

In 2006, the creation of openings in the blind arcade at the rear of the triforium on both sides of the choir for the installation of a new organ showed that the walls had been constructed mainly from Romanesque masonry, probably from the Norman choir, when the choir was rebuilt in the 13th century. The masonry included fragments of attached shafts, double scallop capitals and pieces of interlaced blind arcading. When fully studied these will give us a much better idea of what the Norman cathedral looked like.

Fig. 18 *The east wall of the south transept, showing, at D, the remains of one of the arches of the Norman gallery, above the arch into the John chapel, E. The wall was remodelled in the Perpendicular style.*

Fig. 19 *A pier of three dates — the pier in the south arcade between the 14th-century bays on the left and the two late-12th-century bays on the right, showing the remains of the pier of Wulfstan's church, with banded masonry, in the centre.*

*Fig. 20 Reconstruction of original internal elevation of east wall of the south transept.
(By courtesy of Dr Richard Gem)*

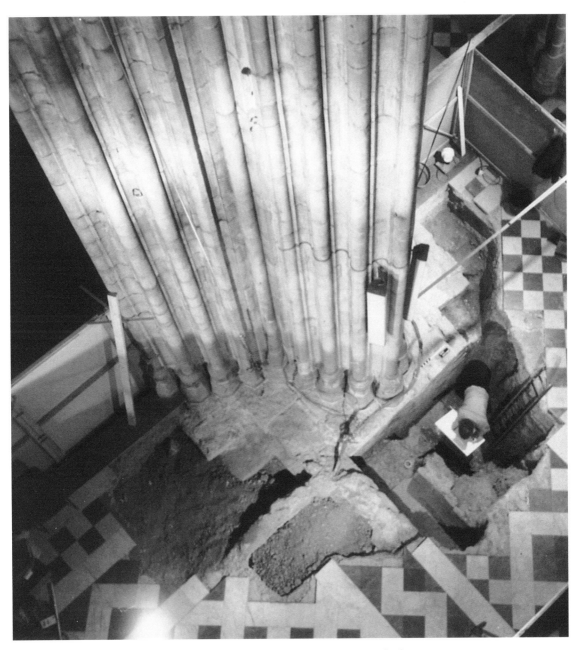

Fig. 21 Excavations at the foot of the central tower of the cathedral.

*Fig. 22 The crypt, showing the later alterations and the sites of excavations.
(Drawn by Chris Guy)*

The Crypt

The crypt is perhaps Worcester's chief glory, in spite of medieval (and more recent) mutilations.

It consists, as can be seen from the plan, (fig. 22), of a nave of seven bays and an apse supported by a forest of free-standing columns with simply decorated cushion capitals.

An ambulatory ran round the central nave but the apsidal end of the ambulatory was blocked-off and filled in during the construction of the new east end and choir in the years after 1224. At the same time, some of the spaces between the original square piers were filled in to give greater support to the new choir above. The filled-in parts can be distinguished from the original piers by their lack of chamfered plinths.

Beyond the ambulatory on the north and south sides were flanking chapels. The eastern end of the southern chapel was rebuilt in the 13th century with a square end and a ribbed vault. The northern chapel was destroyed at an unknown date; it may have been adapted or subsumed into the sacrist's house, which was demolished in the early 18th century and no traces of it are now visible.

Excavations in 1974 showed that there had been a radiating pentagonal chapel on the south side of the apse; excavations for a wheelchair lift in 2006-7 found evidence for a similar chapel to the north. A central chapel, on the east-west axis, is also presumed, although no evidence for this has been seen (fig. 22).

The original doorways into the crypt led from the north and south transepts down short flights of stairs into the crypt's aisles (A, A on fig. 22). These seem to have gone out of use at an early date, perhaps after the

Fig. 23 The crypt.

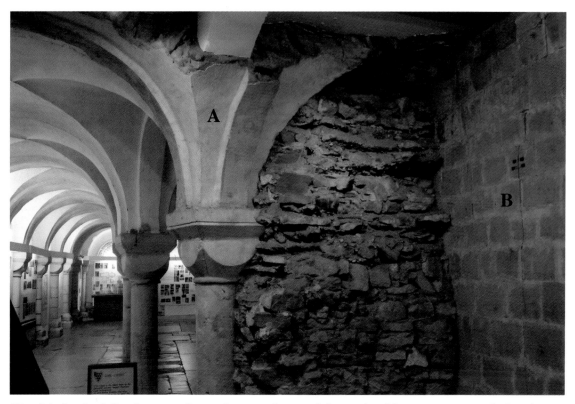

Fig. 24 On the left a free-standing column and part of the vault of the crypt as revealed in the excavation for the new staircase. The soffit, or underside of the transverse arches, A, of the vault, were painted with light orange-red paint, apparently the original decoration of the crypt. In the centre, the blocking wall of c.1230 inserted when the ashlar pier on the right, B, began to crack.

fall of the tower in 1175, being replaced at the south end of the south transept by the present door, B, which is 12th century in character. Presumably there was a door in the similar position on the north side, now obscured by the monument to Bishop Hough.

At the west end of the crypt nave is a round arched opening, G, which appears to have been some form of cupboard. The interior has been badly damaged.

The primary purpose of the crypt was to act as a place of worship and in a monastery with 50 monks many altars would be needed, some of which would have been in the crypt. The documentary evidence shows that there were never shrines in the crypt (as there were in some other churches) although there was an altar dedicated to St Peter. The archaeological evidence also supports the view that there was no shrine in the crypt, as the floor of the ambulatory showed little sign of the wear which would have resulted from the feet of thousands of pilgrims.

Excavations in 1986-87 added information to those of 1974. They showed that two fine ashlar piers, C, C, had been inserted when the new choir was being built and that these were intended to be free-standing and that the ambulatory was to be retained. However large cracks in these piers suggest that serious structural problems were encountered during the building and that it was then that the ambulatory was blocked off and filled in to provide greater support for the choir above,

Fig. 25a and b Capitals in the crypt showing the very thick joints, one packed with lumps of limestone, and the damage and wear which had occurred before the shaft was used.

thus sealing the eastern end of the crypt with whatever chapels and altars it had, and perhaps making the crypt itself largely redundant.

The excavation revealed that the soffits of the transverse arches of the vault had been painted with orange paint and that this was all the decoration the crypt, or at least this part of it, had until the painting of the south side apsidal chapel with simple flowers and false jointing in the late 12th or early 13th century (see fig. 55).

Close examination of the free-standing columns of the crypt shows that many of them were damaged and, more significantly, worn, before being used in the crypt (figs. 25a and b) and that the original mortar overlies the wear. This suggests that they had been reused from an earlier building (as much of the masonry in the eastern slype certainly has) perhaps from St Peter's, whose presbytery was enlarged in *c.*1040 or later. Many of the capitals and abaci are also ill-matched and some show the sort of damage that would occur if they had been removed from another building. While there is general agreement that the columns may have been re-used, there is considerable art-historical resistance to the suggested re-use of the capitals, as there is no recorded use of such capitals in England before the Conquest. Here the art-historical evidence appears to be at odds with the archaeological evidence and the discussion continues.

In 1984 a short shallow trench, D, was dug to investigate the foundations of the free-standing columns in the south aisle (see figs. 27 and 28). This showed, unexpectedly, that the columns did not stand on a sleeper wall or on a concrete raft, but on blocks of rubble which raised the column bases some 23cms. (9ins.) above a concrete raft whose limits could not be seen in such a small trench. One of the rubble fragments used to pack the bases was a segment of Anglo-Saxon architectural ornament (fig. 28), the only piece of

Fig. 26 View of part of the excavation of the crypt ambulatory for the insertion of the new staircase in 1986, showing an attached shaft and base, partly robbed away, and the original whitewashed plaster of the walls, both dating to 1084. Behind is one of the ashlar piers, C, of the new choir of c.1230-1260.

Fig. 27 Base of free-standing pillar in south aisle of crypt, showing rubble packing which raised the base of the pillar above a concrete foundation, perhaps an earlier floor. One of the rubble fragments is a piece of Anglo-Saxon sculpture (fig. 28).

Fig. 28 Photograph of a fragment of Anglo-Saxon sculpture with interlace and a bunch of grapes. Perhaps from a chancel screen. 9th or 10th century.

Anglo-Saxon sculpture yet recovered from the earlier cathedrals. It is datable to the 9th or 10th centuries.

Against the north-eastern wall of the apsidal chapel was found a mortared stone cist (E on fig. 22) containing the disarticulated remains of a man in his forties. Radio-carbon dating of the bones showed that he had died between AD 550 and AD 1030, but most likely in the late 8th or early 9th centuries. He was probably an Anglo-Saxon nobleman, reburied here after his grave was discovered during the original building of the crypt (see the exhibition in the crypt).

Fig. 29 *Elevation of one bay of the chapter house showing the relationship between the Norman windows and the windows which replaced them in the 14th century (from Willis, 1862/63).*

The Chapter House

The Chapter House is in some ways an optical illusion — polygonal and Perpendicular on the outside but circular and Norman within. The Norman work probably dates from 1100-1115 and certainly before 1125, and is the earliest of such circular or polygonal chapter houses, which appear to have been exclusively British — the majority of chapter houses being rectangular, a shape perhaps more suited for their purpose as the daily meeting room for the chapter, with an eastern apse or other focal point for the abbot, which the Worcester room lacks, though it has been suggested that the circular shape is ideal acoustically.

A stone bench (removed in the 17th century to accommodate bookcases) ran round the base of the wall and provided 95 seats, more than ample for the 50 monks of Wulfstan's enlarged monastery. Each seat was backed by a round-headed niche, with above these niches a zone of intersecting blind arcading. This Norman work is patterned in alternate courses of white Cotswold and green Highley stone and is consistent throughout the room and was clearly meant to be seen and therefore was not initially painted or whitened. However, on the northern side of the room there are considerable traces of drapery painted directly on to the stone and covering both the white and green courses, so that at an unknown date, but presumably in medieval times, and perhaps during the 13th-century alterations to the chapter house (see opposite), the banded decoration was effaced. By the 19th century the whole interior had been

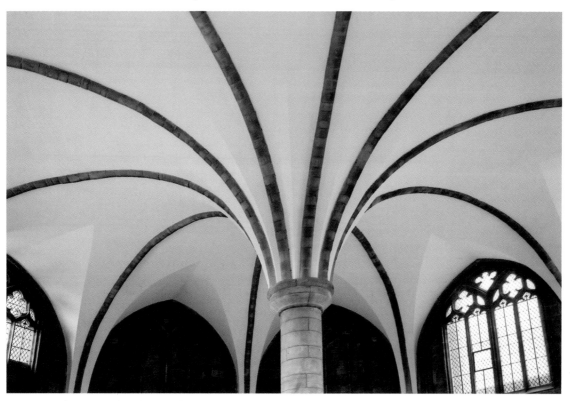

Fig. 30 The central column of the chapter house and the springing of the vault. The capital is typical of Wulfstan's time.

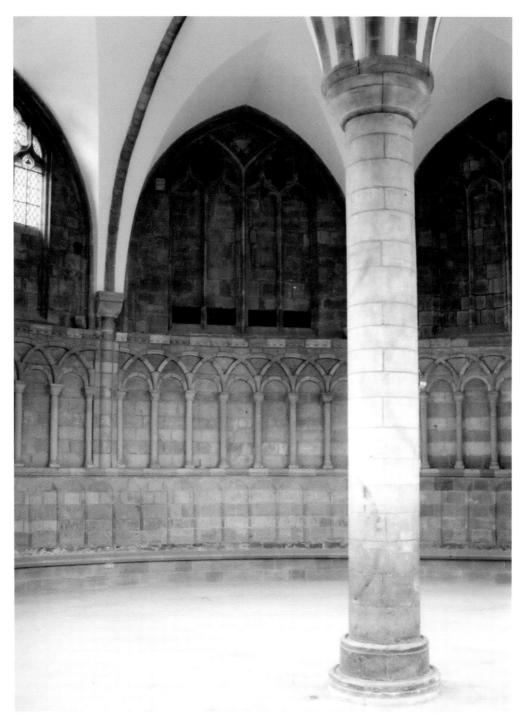

Fig. 31 The interior of the chapter house, showing the central pillar, the base of which was rebuilt in the 13th century, the blind arcading of c.1100-1120 and the blind windows (blind because they abut the rooms over the eastern slype) of the late 14th century. The vault was remodelled at that time to take the enlarged windows.

Fig. 32 The 13th-century 'waterholding' base of the central pillar of the chapter house.

covered in whitewash which was removed in the restoration of the 1860s.

The vault is supported by a central column, and consists of ten radiating semi-circular ribs which stand on slender shafts dividing the outer wall into ten compartments each of which originally contained a single round-headed Norman window. Evidence for one of these has survived the late 14th-century rebuilding and can be seen in the treasury passage to the north (fig. 29). The vault is built mainly of tufa, for lightness, and originally had an elaborate scheme of paintings, now lost, but which are described in a document (MS F81) in the cathedral library (*Worcs. Cath. Notes* etc. 1909-1914 and see below).

Though the design of the chapter house was a *tour de force*, the weight of the vault and its roof gradually thrust out the walls, particularly to the east and south, where they are not supported by adjacent buildings. As a result, the building was remodelled in the late 14th century, although there is some evidence that it may have been extensively repaired before that. The central pillar has a base which is 13th-century rather than Norman in style, and the pillar itself is similar to the 13th-century choir piers in construction. The capital is early Norman and there is a mason's mark on the abacus similar to those found in the niches in the lower part of the wall. Evidence from the 2003 excavation shows that the base was replaced in the 13th century, while post-holes round the pillar suggest that the vault was supported while the work was carried out.

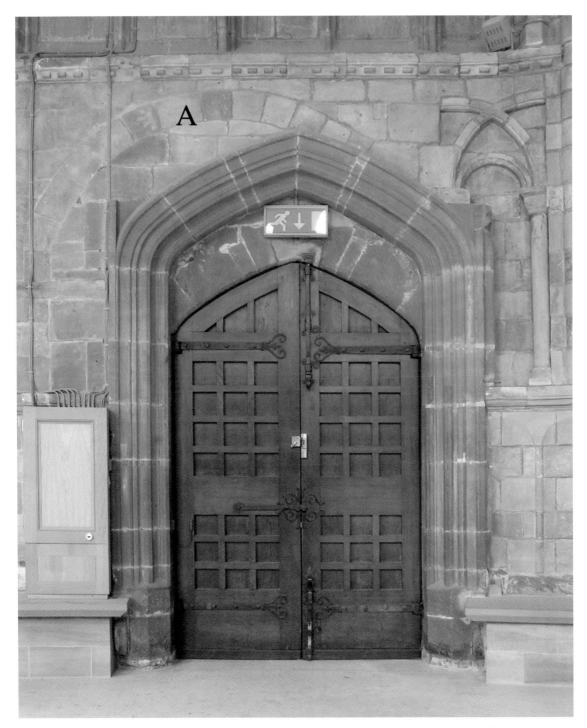

Fig. 33 The door of the chapter house seen from the interior, showing the earlier blocked Norman doorway A, on a different alignment, the new four-centred door being built to fit the vaulting bays of the cloister outside.

Fig. 35 *The groined vault of the eastern slype.*

The Eastern Slype

(T on the front endpaper)

The eastern slype which led through from the cloisters to the monks' cemetery, is a curious anomaly. It lies between the chapter house and the southern wall of the south transept, and so is presumably contemporary with them, yet it is almost entirely built of re-used Anglo-Saxon masonry — bulbous bases, and capitals that appear to be 'lathe-turned', with re-used attached columns — fragments without doubt of one of the Anglo-Saxon churches demolished to make way for Wulfstan's new building. Even the blind arcading is made up of small re-used voussoirs crudely put together, while the string course between the arcade sections comprises re-used abacuses. Only the capitals on the south side, which are similar to those in the crypt, appear to be new but even they could be re-used. While the demolished earlier churches were undoubtedly re-used as rubble or re-cut as ashlar in Wulfstan's church, these are the only fragments that are visible. The ledge on which the blind arcading stands is equally irregular with a chamfered plinth in two places but rough

Fig. 34 *(Left) Detail of the blind arcade of the eastern slype showing a re-used Anglo-Saxon capital and base.*

Fig. 36 The northern blind arcade of the eastern slype showing the re-used Anglo-Saxon voussoirs, capitals and bases.

uncoursed masonry elsewhere. The whole passage is very different in construction from the other surviving parts of Wulfstan's church, but the explanation is probably now beyond recovery.

The east walk of the cloister includes two large rectangular recesses, at present housing the redundant bells, which probably held cupboards for the books being used by the monks working in the cloister scriptorium, while the west walk includes the monks' lavatorium or wash-place. This was fed by a lead pipe, over 2,000 yards long, which brought water across the river from the Henwick road. This lavatorium has clearly been reset at some time since the ends of the water trough are now blocked off by the 14th-century vaulting shafts with a third shaft inserted half way along its length. A trough or drain probably ran against the back wall with a shelf in front, the reverse of the present situation.

The Monastic Buildings

The monastic buildings are outside the scope of this book, except to draw attention to the ruins of the dormitory, its undercroft and its reredorter (or latrine) with a deep drain which emptied into the river. These buildings, together with the infirmary, which has completely disappeared, lay between the west end of the cathedral and the river. This westerly site was an unusual position for the dormitory which normally lay over the chapter house on the eastern range of the cloister, with a night staircase giving access to the south transept for the first service of the day. The unusual shape of the chapter house with its conical roof precluded this, and Worcester's monks had to walk the whole length of the nave to get to their choir.

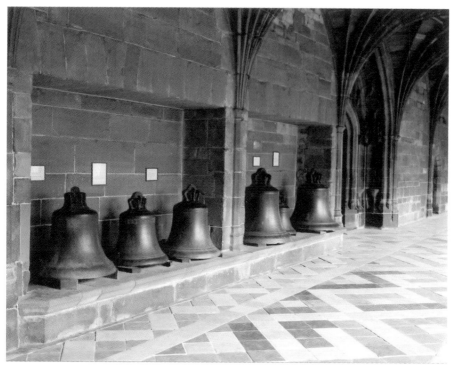

Fig. 37 The east walk of the cloister, showing the cupboard recesses, now housing redundant bells. The monastic library was probably here until the mid-14th century when it was moved to its present position.

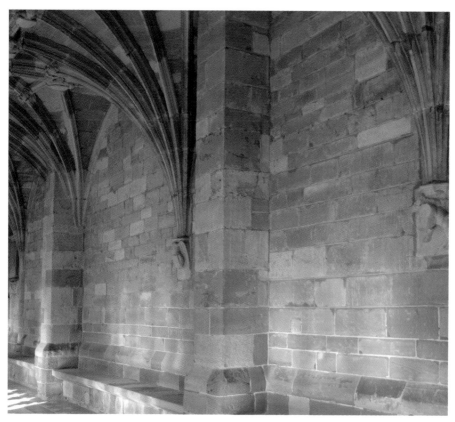

Fig. 38 The north wall of the cloister — the outside of the south wall of the nave — showing the massive plain buttresses. Note that the late 14th-century vaulting bays of the cloisters are spaced in an entirely different rhythm.

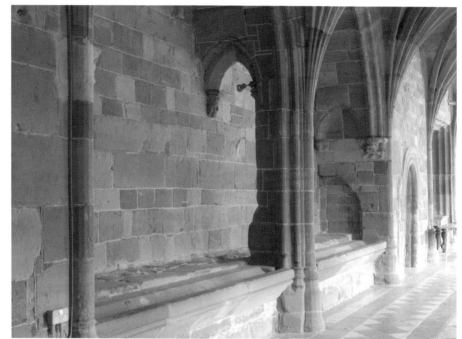

Fig. 39 The cloister west walk with the lavatorium in the foreground. This has been rebuilt as the water trough is cut across by the 14th-century pier for the cloister vault and its ends are blocked off.

Fig. 40 The refectory from the east end showing the Norman undercroft with its flat buttresses and small round-headed windows. The corner buttresses are additions of the 14th century and the east wall has an inserted late 14th-century window with flowing tracery.

Fig. 41 Christ in Majesty. A great sculptured panel of the early 13th century at the east end of the monastic refectory (College Hall) showing the seated Christ in a mandorla, a lobed oval space, surrounded by the symbols of the four Evangelists and flanked by niches which presumably held figures of saints. There are traces of paint, particularly red paint, in the backgrounds. It was hacked flat after the Reformation, perhaps at the same time as the same treatment to the reredos in Prince Arthur's chantry. The friezes above and below are of the 14th century.

The Refectory

The refectory (now called College Hall) takes up the whole of the south range of the cloisters. It was originally a Norman first floor hall of great size standing on an undercroft, which still exists, though much altered. The undercroft has flat buttresses and small round-headed windows to the south, and has a groined vault supported by a central row of squat piers. The three central piers are cylindrical with simple capitals suggesting that these central bays had a different function from the two ends.

The north wall, that is, the cloister wall, is very thick with buttresses of two sizes, and with two large blocked Norman arches. The main 14th-century doorway into the hall is here, towards the west end, while there is a smaller doorway into the undercroft, which has been extensively remodelled in this area.

In medieval times, the original doorway into the undercroft appears to be that still existing in the southern slype leading into the cloisters.

The doorway into College Hall on the south side, though 14th century in style, is

Fig. 42 The undercroft of the refectory showing the rough vaulting which has lost its original plastering. This would have been similar to that which survives in the eastern slype. Two of the apparent scalloped capitals are fragments of decorated string-courses.

new work of the 19th century and excavations there in 1992 have shown that it partly blocks an original Norman window and that there was no door here at ground level in Norman times, though there may have been one subsequently at the level of the hall, reached by a wooden staircase, to give access to the kitchen.

The hall itself was entirely rebuilt or drastically remodelled in the 14th century, but it was also extensively modified in the 19th century so that much of the original work is obscured; it is possible that the upper walls are basically Norman. It is hard to see why the building should have been dismantled down to the top of the undercroft without very good

reason, and this is not apparent, though it has been suggested that the original upper floor here (and of other buildings, such as the infirmary), may have been of timber or timber-framed, perhaps with stone gable walls.

Inside the east end of the hall are the mutilated remains of a magnificent over-life-size Christ in Majesty surrounded by the symbols of the Evangelists (fig. 41). The date of this is *c*.1220-1230, that is, the date of the beginning of the rebuilding of the east end of the cathedral, though the friezes above and below are 14th-century additions. This great sculpture was presumably built into the east end of the Norman refectory and re-used and re-framed when the hall was remodelled.

A survey of the undercroft shows that it is a very complex building which appears to subsume three earlier buildings on slightly different alignments. This may account for the fact that it is some 5° out of alignment with the rest of the cathedral complex. The stone vault appears to have been built in a second phase, supported on added internal walls, and presumably replacing a wooden ceiling. The external casing with its row of small round-headed windows is probably later rather than early 12th century in date, and contemporary with the doorway into the cloisters at the east end.

4. The Later 12th Century

The work on Wulfstan's original plan for the monastery appears to have continued until at least the end of the first quarter of the 12th century and perhaps beyond.

However, in 1175 there was an event which, however interpreted, marked a setback and caused considerable rebuilding. An entry in the *Worcester Annals* under that year says: *Nova turris Wigorniae corruit*, 'The new tower of Worcester fell'.

This laconic comment poses some difficulties, principally the position of the fallen tower. Willis thought it was the crossing tower, but Brakspear suggested that the tower which fell was one of a pair at the west end and the opinion is still divided. However, the excavations at the foot of each crossing tower pier, made in the 1980s to examine the foundations before the tower's restoration,

showed unequivocally that there had been a second tower, sandwiched in time between Wulfstan's original tower and the present 14th-century tower (see figs. 43, 45, 46). This makes it extremely probable that it was the central tower which fell in 1175 and was

Fig. 44 A bay of the late 12th-century west end of the cathedral.

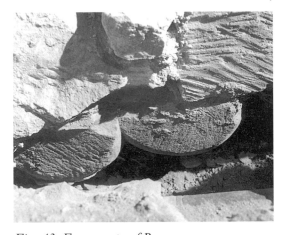

Fig. 43 Fragments of Romanesque masonry, including a double capital (e on fig. 45), used as rubble in the foundation of the second tower, c.1175-1200, and discovered in the excavation of the south-west tower pier in 1981.

Worcester Cathedral — south-west tower pier, north-east angle. Interpretation

Scale in feet

Fig. 45 Axonometric drawing of the excavation of the south-west tower pier. The excavation at the base of the pier showed conclusively that there were three phases of construction: first, a massive base of uncoursed rubble, clearly, for reasons which there is not space to detail here, the Norman foundations of c.1084. On this stood a foundation which, at first sight, appeared to have a chamfered plinth of Norman date and to be contemporary with the base below. However, closer examination showed that the stones of which it was constructed (d) were, in fact, reused abaci from capitals or string courses paralleled exactly in the nearby crypt of 1084, but here reused upside down. Mortar samples were taken from joints at a and b, examined and compared and shown to be different from one another. Mortar samples from joints in the 14th-century pier at c were also examined and proved to be different again. Clearly there were three phases of construction. However, it was also seen that the 14th-century pier, which was a different shape from the underlying bases, had itself been packed with reused Norman architectural fragments, including a column drum, f, and a double capital, e. g is a floor, probably of the first period, which has sunk and tilted, while h is a posthole, perhaps for a scaffold pole, set in pit i. The probable sequence of events is thus: the building of the first Norman tower, I, after 1084 and perhaps as late as 1150s; the collapse of this tower and building, after 1175, of a second tower, II, on foundations derived from the collapsed masonry; the building of the third tower, III, in the late 14th century, again reusing Norman masonry, but this time probably from the destruction of the ambulatory of the crypt when the east end of the cathedral was rebuilt in the 13th century.

Fig. 46 The foundation of the south-west tower pier. Compare with the drawing above.

Fig. 47 One of the capitals of the late 12th-century western bays of the nave, showing the awkward adaptation of the triple-shafted capital to the attached column of the 11th-century pier (in white) below. Beyond, on the right, are the shafts and capitals of the 14th-century nave arcade (cf. Fig 71).

renewed, incorporating re-used Romanesque masonry, soon afterward, eventually being replaced in the 14th century.

However, why should a tower which fell in 1175 be called the *nova turris*, since Wulfstan's original tower was presumably built soon after 1084? One possible answer to this question is that the original tower was squat, rising only a little higher than the surrounding roofs, and that the 'new tower' had been a heightening of the first tower and it was this addition, made a short while before 1175, that had collapsed. This would fit the excavated evidence. It has been objected that there is too much original Romanesque masonry surviving at the west end of the choir for it to have been the central tower which collapsed, but if it were only a low tower being heightened it may (as with other towers, notably at Chichester) have collapsed vertically, falling inwards on itself and doing little damage to the surrounding masonry.

Fig. 48 The triforium of the two late 12th-century western bays, showing the stepped arches with zig-zag decoration in the centre and the curious applied whorls, resembling cake decoration, called paterae. Notice the mixture of round and pointed arches in this transitional style of c.1175-1200.

The transept first floors nearer the crossing may well have been damaged or destroyed when the tower fell. There was undoubtedly remodelling of the transepts at about this time with the removal of the galleries and the chapels opening out of them at first floor level.

For example, surviving fragments of later 12th-century work can be seen in the south transept and there are splendid ornate late 12th-century blind windows in the same transept's south wall, though these are now barely visible behind the case of the great organ.

The argument that it was one of a pair of western towers which fell in 1175 has been supported by the fact that the two western bays of the cathedral were completely rebuilt at about that time, a date based on stylistic grounds. Whatever the force of the argument, it is clear from the architectural evidence that these two bays replace two earlier bays and were not an extension to the nave. First, the two piers (B, B on the front endpaper) are each of three phases, the northern and southern shafts part of Wulfstan's church of

the 11th century; the western shafts of the late 12th century and the eastern shafts of the 14th century. It can be seen that the 11th-century shafts are semi-circular and therefore must have been part of a pier and not part of a western wall. It is also worth commenting that the use of white and green stone in these piers is not consistent, as it is in the chapter house, which suggests that here as well as in

Fig. 49 One of the high capitals of the two late 12th-century western bays of the nave.

Fig. 50 The scalloped trumpet capitals of the late 12th-century piers of the two western bays of the nave, a logical development of the capitals in the crypt. Notice the imaginative variety of the designs and the way in which the concave abaci and the undercut trumpet shapes enhance the play of light and shade on the capitals.

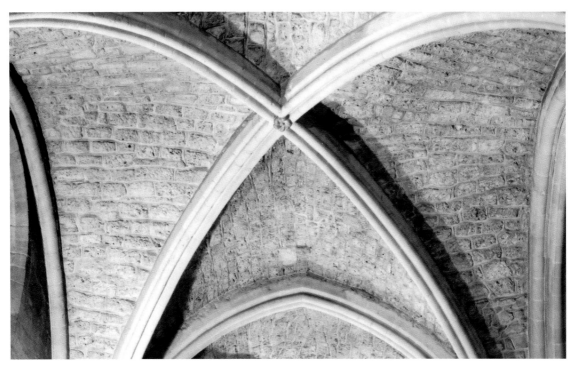

Fig. 51 The late 12th-century vault of the two western bays of the south aisle showing the mixture of round and pointed arches of this transitional period. The vault between the ribs would have been plastered and whitewashed — the present rustic appearance with careful pointing is 19th century.

other parts of the early Norman church which have survived, where the stonework is equally random, it was not meant to be seen but was white-washed.

The two western bays, built as they were in the last quarter of the 12th century, and perhaps as early as 1175+, are 'Transitional' in the sense that they combine round-headed and slightly pointed arches in the same design (for instance, the triple clerestory arches are pointed-round-pointed). The early Norman gallery or tribune has been replaced by a narrow triforium, blocked off from the roof space behind except for doors in the centre of each bay, and with a tripartite arrangement of

Fig. 52 The exterior of the late 12th-century bays of the nave showing, at A, a blocked Norman window, possibly circular, replaced by a curvilinear Decorated window, renewed in the 19th century.

Fig. 53 The late 12th-century west door, largely rebuilt in the 19th-century refurbishment. The masonry of the 12th century in the lower parts of the doorways can be distinguished from the 19th-century masonry by its different tooling. The wooden boxes at A, A cover the fragments of the 11th-century bases which prove that the west door of Wulfstan's church was here and of the same width.

Fig. 54 The 12th-century door at the east end of the refectory which opens into the southern slype leading from College Green to the cloister.

semi-circular arches, zigzag decorated, with the central arch stilted, all contained within a pointed arch. The blank spaces within the arches are filled with individual paterae curiously shaped like whorls of cake icing.

The main arches of these two bays are slightly but elegantly pointed and the capitals throughout are variations on the trumpet scallop and crocket types, except for the capitals on the high vaulting shafts, which are richly decorated with foliage, one (fig. 49) harking back to the original Corinthian capital from which these capitals ultimately derive. They are hardly appreciated without binoculars.

The ribbed vaulting in the corresponding two bays of the south aisle is contemporary and very fine; it is probable that the compartments, or severies, between the ribs were once plastered and whitened also. In the south wall are two simple blind round-headed windows, which were probably matched by real windows in the north aisle. However, this aisle and its windows were largely rebuilt in the 14th century, though the wall shafts were retained.

5. THE PAINTED DECORATION OF THE LATER 12TH AND 13TH CENTURIES

So far as we can tell the interior of Wulfstan's church was plain and white, as the crypt and the eastern slype are now, with the only evidence for added decoration the orange paint on the soffits or undersides of the arches in the crypt, and some fragments of plaster with red parallel lines which may be from the upper parts of the church. If the windows were of plain glass (and there is no evidence at present of stained glass here at this date) the building would be full of reflected light, much more like a vast nonconformist chapel than the present interior, which depends for its decoration on the light and shade of modelled and sculptured stone, some of which was itself originally painted.

However, it is now clear that in the later 12th and early 13th centuries the interior of Wulfstan's church was transformed by great schemes of wall and vault paintings. Some still survive fragmentarily on the walls, for others we have archaeological evidence, while for some we have only documentary evidence.

The chief evidence for the decoration in the main body of the cathedral comes from the large quantity of painted plaster debris found in the crypt excavations of 1986-87, while we have documentary evidence for the schemes in the chapter house, and the 'Maccabees' series.

However, these colourful paintings do not seem to have survived for very long, being swept away in the rebuilding of the east end in the years after 1224, in the probable rebuilding of the chapter house vault, and in general the change from areas of whitened wall and vault which formed an ideal support for paintings, to a multiplicity of columns, much larger window space and a new emphasis on light and shade which left little room for painting except on the vaults.

We do not know what decorative schemes there were on the Norman tower and nave piers and walls but they may have been extensive, eventually being destroyed in the 14th and 15th centuries when the tower and nave were rebuilt.

In addition to the still visible remains of wall paintings, traces of paint can be seen on the sculptured figures which fill the spandrels of both the choir and nave triforia. The backgrounds against which they sit have also been painted, apparently with washes of red. No doubt many other sculptures as well as these were painted or gilded.

The Victorian scraping was ruthless and must have removed much still extant painting though some bosses have since been repainted and re-gilded.

In 1995-96 staff and postgraduate students of the Courtauld Institute of Art carried out a detailed survey of all the medieval polychromy in the cathedral. The survey revealed a quite unexpected amount of painting surviving on walls, on sculpture and on carved decoration. In addition to the examples already mentioned, there are extensive remains of important paintings in the east and west wall arcades of the south-east transept — haloed figures, including a probable Virgin and Child — and fragments, one the carefully drawn outline of an ear, of two figures at the northern end of the east wall.

One of the most exciting finds was in the arcading of the north wall of the lady chapel, where the 'ghosts' of several shields can just be made out. They appear to be 13th century in date, and if they are contemporary with the chapel, *c*.1224, they are extremely important, since they would pre-date the earliest similar examples in a major building — those in the arcade of the choir aisles at Westminster Abbey.

Close examination of the sculptures in the spandrels of the nave and choir triforia show that they still carry remains of their original painting. Both the carving and the polychromy of the 14th-century figures in the nave are rather crude, but their 13th-century counterparts in the choir are of superb quality,

with splendid polychromy including gilding. David Park, who led the Courtauld survey, goes so far as saying that 'they are unquestionably among the finest polychromed sculptures of their period in England' and deserve comparison with the better known, slightly later, sculpture of the Angel Choir at Lincoln.

Wall paintings in the Norman church

As we have seen, the original decoration of the crypt was shown by the 1986-87 excavation of the staircase to be simply orange paint on the soffits of the transverse arches. The excavation of the apsidal chapel revealed, however, that it had been decorated with false jointing and flowers with curving stalks (fig. 55). A 13th-century date is suggested for this

Fig. 55 Wall painting, probably of the late 12th or early 13th centuries, in the southern apsidal chapel of the crypt, uncovered by the excavations for the new staircase here. It consists of wide false-jointing with simple flowers and thin stems. The blank area in the centre of the photograph is perhaps the site of an altar, or a memorial. As can be seen, the false jointing on either side is not aligned.

painting by parallels with very similar decoration in the chancel of Martley Church, 6 miles away, where the decoration continues into the splay of a pointed and therefore presumably 13th-century window. However, since this end of the crypt was destroyed in *c.*1240 for the building of the new choir, the painting must have been carried out only shortly before it became redundant. There are similar paintings, with single flowers, on the capitals at the entrance to the chapel at its western angle, though these are now difficult to discern.

During the excavations for the construction of the new staircase into the crypt the tons of rubble which filled its abandoned east end were carefully sorted and a large quantity of painted wall plaster was recovered from the lowest levels of the filling, plaster which with very little doubt was derived from the destruction of the Norman chancel above.

Determined attempts have been made to fit together these many fragments, with comparatively little success, since presumably they represent only a very little small proportion of the total original paintings. However, some clues to the decorative schemes can be deduced and these will be published in due course, but undoubtedly the most important fragment is the face of a saint or angel (fig. 56). This extraordinarily beautiful painting has been provisionally dated to the later 12th century. It is remarkable for the reflection in the eye and the sensitivity of the mouth which go beyond the stylisation of much contemporary painting. It is perhaps related to a now lost painting of an angel with a censer, which was found on the jamb of a window in the crypt 'destroyed to make way for the

Fig. 56 (Top) Fragment of wall painting found in the crypt excavations of 1986-87.

Fig. 57 (Lower) An angel with a censer. Copy of a wall painting found in the crypt in 1860.

new foundations' in 1860. This angel was copied at full size and in colour before being destroyed but the copy has recently and very unfortunately disappeared, though not before being photographed (fig. 57).

Two Lunettes

On the north wall of the western end of the southern crypt chapel are two painted lunettes so badly damaged as to be almost indecipherable (F, F on fig. 22). The more westerly of the two has traces of two figures, the right-hand one a bishop with the lettering S.TOMAS — presumably St Thomas à Becket rather than the doubting disciple. Other letters are faintly discernible, suggesting that the left-hand figure is St Peter. The other lunette is more badly damaged but the outline of a trefoil filling the space and therefore framing whatever was painted in it, can clearly be seen. The trefoil dates the painting to the early 13th century. Again two bishops seem to have been depicted.

The Chapter House

In the cathedral library there is a manuscript, F81, a 12th-century folio of St Jerome, on the fly leaf of which is a series of verses entitled *Versus Capituli*, implying that they were inscribed in a chapter house, and since the manuscript apparently originated in Worcester, probably the chapter house here.

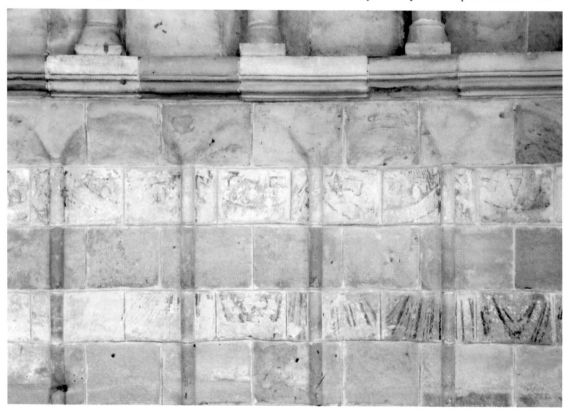

Fig. 58 The traces of painting in the niches of the chapter house seating, of busts of angels holding closed books above swags of drapery. Note that the painting has been applied directly to the stone (without plastering) and that it crosses the banded stonework which had originally been intended to be seen.

A transcription of the verses will be found in James, 1913 and a translation will be found in Wilson, 1913 (both in *Worcs. Cath. Notes* etc. 1909-1914). There are ten verses, which correspond to the ten bays of the chapter house, and they are preceded by a set of lines headed in *circuitu domus*, which Wilson suggests were painted 'in rather large capitals on a band of stonework running all round the Chapter House, and probably below the paintings …' (where there would have been space before the windows were enlarged in the 14th-century rebuilding).

The subjects were taken from the Old and New Testaments and were arranged in symbolic groups. By remarkable coincidence there is an illuminated manuscript in the library of Eton College, which contains a series of pages containing roundels, with verses round their edges, ten of which coincide almost exactly with the Worcester verses (Henry, 1991). It seems very likely therefore that the Worcester chapter house was painted with roundels very similar, if not identical, to those in the Eton College manuscript, though there are five roundels and two separate half-roundels on each page of the manuscript, whereas the Worcester manuscript describes only four roundels to each 'bay'. It is suggested that each compartment of the ten-sided vault contained four roundels, disposed as in the accompanying sketch by Brakspear who suggested this arrangement. This seems highly likely as there is no other space for them, even though the niches behind the encircling bench were eventually painted, though clearly not with roundels. An article by Heslop published in 2001 suggests that the chapter house was deliberately designed to be decorated with the ten groups of roundels and that the Eton manuscript and objects decorated with similar scenes are derived from it. It would be possible, using the Eton College manuscript as a model, to reconstruct in colour the vault of the chapter house here as it was in the later 12th century — it must have been spectacular.

Of the niches (fig. 58), Willis wrote 'On the wall of the niches were traces of painting, of which black outlines remained. They were exactly the same in each niche, and represented an angel holding an expanded mantle, as in the old paintings of the stalls of St Stephen's Chapel, Westminster, but these figures were simpler, showing merely the head and part of the wings, with the hands above the mantle. As the niches are 4 feet high above the seat, the head and hands of the guardian angel would just appear over the head and shoulders of each monk when seated in his stall.'

There are also faint traces of painting on the central pillar, notably two bands, forming ovals on the east and west faces and lozenges on the north and south. Close scrutiny reveals a stem or branch emerging from one of the bands on the east face and remains of figures on the north face, suggesting that the Tree of Jesse was painted on the column.

A Maccabees Cycle

In 1914 Canon Wilson drew attention to a manuscript in the library of Clare College, Cambridge MS KK5.6, on a fly-leaf of which, in handwriting of about the first half of the 13th century, is a series of Latin verses describing pictures illustrating the story of the Maccabees (Wilson, 1914 in *Worcs. Cath. Notes* etc. 1909-1914).

Wilson argues that the scheme of paintings described on the above MS was on the vault and perhaps also on the south wall of the western slype, (now, in 2007, the cathedral gift shop). Though there is no proof of this, Wilson saw traces of paint along the ribs of the vault before they were removed by workmen without further record (on 17 September 1914). It is possible, however, that these paintings which he describes as 'scenes of war and bloodshed' may have been in the Guesten Hall (e.g. see p.65 below) or in the refectory or the cloisters.

6.   THE NEW EAST END

King John died at Newark in 1216 and, following a request made in a codicil to his will, his body was brought to Worcester and buried before the high altar. Two years later the church, completed after the rebuilding of the two western bays and the collapsed central tower, was dedicated in the presence of the young King Henry III, and the body of St Wulfstan was translated into a shrine.

It is surprising, therefore, that only six years later, in 1224, Bishop William of Blois with his master mason, Alexander, replanned the whole east end, beginning with the construction of the lady chapel and eastern transepts outside the Norman apse in the monks' graveyard, followed by the demolition and rebuilding of the Norman chancel.

The reasons for this drastic remodelling are not clear but may be connected with the promotion of the cult of St Wulfstan and the encouragement of pilgrimages to his shrine and to that of St Oswald, which lay together, with King John's tomb between them. (It is suggested by Mr Michael Craze that John's tomb and the two saints' shrines lay along the axis of the church rather than laterally).

Fig. 59 The east end of the cathedral with the south-eastern transept and Prince Arthur's chantry on the right.

Fig. 60 The south-east transept which illustrates the 'unrestrained verticalism' of which Pevsner speaks (1968 p.302). Attached Purbeck marble shafts run from the top of the blind arcade straight through to the vault, only punctuated by the annular rings which attach the shafts to the structure.

Fig. 61 The vault of the lady chapel and the eastern transepts crossing (painted by Hardman in the 19th-century restoration).

There is also the recorded collapse of two small towers in 1222. Although the positions of these towers are not known, if they were at the east end, they may have weakened the structure or destroyed sufficient of it to suggest total rebuilding.

The new design removed the galleries of the Norman east end and replaced them with triforia. Since the galleries had almost certainly contained altars, space for these could now be found in the extended eastern arm and the new transepts.

The work on the new building began in 1224 and may have continued until 1240-1250. William of Blois died in 1236 and was succeeded by Walter de Cantaloupe who continued the work on the choir. There is a visible break in the construction between that part — the lady chapel and the eastern transepts — which lay outside the Norman building and the part which replaced the Norman chancel and apse. Willis describes the differences in the design of these two parts in detail (*op. cit.* 1863). It is at the junction of the two phases of construction that problems arose which resulted in the demolition and filling in of the ambulatory of the crypt (p.22 above). The creation of openings in the

Fig. 62 The north arcade of the lady chapel. The blind arcade at the back of the triforium has spacing which is out of step with the arcade at the front. Purbeck marble is used throughout for free-standing, clustered and attached shafts of great delicacy.

blind arcade at the back of the triforium in the choir in 2006 showed that much masonry from the Norman choir was recycled for use in the 13th century. On the north side several 13th-century capitals are cut from the blocks of Norman capitals.

The new east end is in the Early English style with pointed arches, tall narrow windows, a marvellous variety of stiff-leaf capitals, (which contrast sharply with the plainness of the previous Norman capitals) and the use of black Purbeck marble shafts to contrast with the Highley stone used in the rest of the building (figs. 59-62).

The arcades, triforia and clerestories of this new building were different in their propor-

tions from the Norman chancel, as can be seen from the fragments of the earlier church which remain (fig. 63), and as Willis points out, the lady chapel arcades are narrower and higher than those of the choir (because the choir floor has to be higher over the crypt) giving 'the Lady Chapel ... a grandeur and loftiness of appearance greatly superior to that of the choir, whose arches appear sprawling in comparison ...'.

The emphasis is on verticality throughout. To quote another enthusiastic admirer of this building, 'what conveys that irresistible excelsior to the Lady Chapel and the Transepts is that, though the windows are in two tiers, Purbeck shafts run up all the way' (Pevsner, 1968, 303).

Fig. 63 Plans of the Norman crypt and the 13th-century choir superimposed to show their relationship.

The ribbed vault has longitudinal as well as transverse ribs and the painted scheme throughout is by Hardman (fig. 64). The two eastern transepts and the lady chapel have blank pointed-trefoil arcading running round the whole east end, but this does not continue westward into the choir aisles. The capitals of this blind arcading are all stiff-leaf crockets and the spandrels contain sculpture of great variety: foliage, little animals and monsters and figures and, most interestingly, little religious scenes: The Angel sounding the Last trump; the Resurrection, with the dead climbing out of their graves; the Expulsion from Paradise; the Tortures of Hell; the Annunciation; the Visitation and the Nativity (fig. 65). One of the sculptures in the north

aisle shows William of Blois offering a model of his new church to an altar in an act of dedication (fig. 66).

Much of the extreme east end was rebuilt in the Early English style by Perkins in the 1860s as part of the great refurbishment, restoring to it something of the unity it must have had in the 13th century (see chapter 9 below).

We can try to envisage the cathedral as it was when the new east end was completed — the new choir was attached to the second Norman tower and the transepts, though modified, were still Norman; the main part of the nave was probably still as it was in Wulfstan's time, though perhaps with painted decoration and the two western bays were late

Fig. 64 Part of the vault of the choir, painted by Hardman. The panel of blind arcading on the left was painted by Helen Lubin to fill an area left blank by renewal of the plaster.

Fig. 65 (Left) The blind arcading of the south eastern transept (the dean's chapel) showing one of the spandrel sculptures — the Expulsion of Adam and Eve from Paradise.

Fig. 66 (Below) Sculpture in a spandrel of the north aisle of the lady chapel, c.1224, very probably representing Bishop William of Blois presenting his newly rebuilt church at an altar. However, while the trefoil in the gable of the church and the cusped doorway behind him are 13th century in style, all the windows are round-headed, i.e. Norman and therefore anachronistic. The southern of the tomb effigies on either side of the altar in the lady chapel has a similar beard and moustache, and is also probably William of Blois, though there is confusion, in both the labelling and the literature, between him and the northern effigy, which is almost certainly earlier, and therefore not Walter de Cantelupe, who did not become bishop until 1237 and died in 1266, then being buried before the high altar.

Norman, as they are now (see fig. 44). It was probably not a coincidence that Worcester's great Antiphoner, including music going back to Oswald's episcopate, was collected together at this time, the building of the new choir.

Figs. 67 a to e. A series of crocket and stiff leaf capitals from the east end of the cathedral. As the building progressed from east to west the capitals became increasingly complex eventually becoming smaller and more naturalistic in the crossing and the nave (figs. 69 and 71a and b).

Fig. 68 The east end of the cathedral showing the way in which Perkins married his new east end with the original 13th-century arcade of the lady chapel.

7.   THE 14TH AND 15TH CENTURIES

Fig. 69 The north arcade of the nave, started c.1317-20, seen from the west. The vault was added c.1377.

After the completion of the choir, probably by the middle of the 13th century, there seems to have been a pause in the rebuilding until *c*.1317-20 when a start was made on rebuilding the north arcade of the nave and the north aisle in the Decorated style, with flowing tracery in the windows (especially elaborate in the Jesus chapel) and with complex piers with capitals of leaves more bunched and realistic than the stiff-leaf capitals of the lady chapel and the eastern parts of the choir's, but seeming to develop from the capitals of the choir's western piers.

It is possible that the south wall of the nave (which is also the north wall of the cloister) and part of the north wall of the refectory may have been rebuilt in the period between *c*.1260 and 1320. Although these walls appear to be Norman there are compelling arguments for them to be of the late 13th or early 14th century, since the lower parts of the windows had to be filled in when the cloister vaults were inserted and the rhythm of the bays is totally different.

Fig. 70   The tierceron vault of the nave, built c.*1377.*

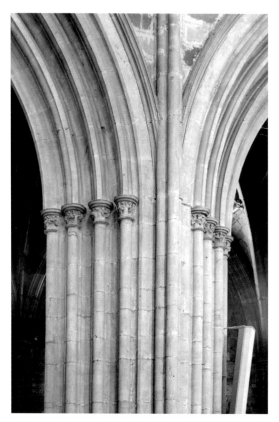

Fig. 71a (left) shows one of the Decorated capitals of the nave arcade with continuous abaci and bold clustered leaves, in comparison with the Perpendicular capitals in b (right) which are separate and smaller allowing the mouldings to run up between them, emphasising the verticality of the design.

At least the Jesus chapel and the two eastern bays of the north aisle were vaulted by Bishop Thomas Cobham, *c*.1327. The triforium and clerestory of bays 3 and 4 (counting from the west) are in the Perpendicular style as is the whole of the southern arcade and aisle vault and the windows in the south wall. Here the bases are different from those on the north and the capitals are separate and of thinner leaves. The building break on the north side may have been the result of the Black Death in the late 1340s and is now visible on the north side of the triforium wall, within the aisle roof space.

In spite of the time between the rebuilding of the north and south arcades of the nave, which span the transition between the Decorated and Perpendicular periods, the styles of the two arcades, though subtly different, are sufficiently similar to preserve the unity of the whole. Whether this is due to innate conservatism on the part of the Worcester masons, or a conscious desire to unify the design, we have no way of knowing.

During the rebuilding of the nave and the aisles, the Norman roof, which was presumably of wood, not vaulted in stone, must have been removed and the nave left open to the sky until both arcades were completed, when it was vaulted in 1377. (It is, of course, possible that the roof was completed some years before the vault was begun.). This was at the same time as the building of the library, in the south

Fig. 72 The north range of the cloister and the external wall of the south aisle with the windows of the library above. The window tracery of the cloister is 19th century, by Perkins, the aisle windows are late 14th-century Perpendicular of an elaborate kind, while the rectangular two-light windows above are of the mid-15th century, probably of the time of Bishop Carpenter, (1444-1476) to give more light to the library.

nave aisle roof space, and the dormitory (now destroyed). Analysis of the nave roof timbers suggests that the two western bays may have been roofed before the rebuilding of the remainder of the nave. These two bays may therefore have remained in use, although how they were supported is unknown.

Meanwhile in 1320 Prior Braunston built the Guesten Hall; the Edgar Tower was completed in 1368-69; the refectory and the cloister rebuilt (on Norman foundations) in 1372, and the tower built (or begun) in 1374 and its vault over the crossing constructed in 1376. In 1378 the Water Gate was built and in 1379 the infirmary and the choir stalls; in 1380 the west window (now, of course, replaced) and in 1386 the north porch.

A recent survey of the Edgar Tower (the great gate) shows that it was a residential tower of high status with vaulted chambers in each turret and a great hall, used as a court-house, above the gateway. Built into one of the interior walls are sections of chevron ornament reused presumably from an earlier Norman gate. A detailed survey of the tower is proposed.

Fig. 73 The interior of the library, built in 1377, fenestrated in the mid-15th century.

In addition, at some time in the late 14th century, the chapter house was drastically remodelled, with new, enlarged windows of early Perpendicular style between deep thin buttresses (fig. 90). The external surface of the thick Norman wall was cut away and refaced, reducing the weight of the walls, and the vaults over the windows changed from low and semi-circular to high and pointed, transferring the thrust of the vault on to the new buttresses.

This remarkable and very costly spate of building began in *c.*1317 and went on for 70 years. The dates given here may be the dates at which the work was begun, or on which they ended, since such a programme must have meant overlapping work on the major contracts, but whichever they are, they give the relative chronology and enable us to see how the work alternated between the monastic buildings and the church, culminating in the north porch.

It is worth pointing out that the quality of the Guesten Hall and the refectory show that the monastic buildings were as architecturally important and imposing as the cathedral itself.

In 1504 Prince Arthur's chantry was constructed, the last addition to the cathedral church before the dissolution of the monastery.

Fig. 74 The east face of the Edgar Tower, the entrance to the monastic precinct. Originally built in the 14th century (completed in 1368-69) it was heavily restored in the 19th century refurbishment. The statues date from the early 20th century but the great wooden doors are original.

The Tower

As we have seen, the present tower is the third on the same foundations. We know little about the second tower, except that it was based on the foundations built for Wulfstan's tower, but packed with re-used Romanesque masonry.

The third, present tower, that of 1374, has piers which are diamond shaped in plan and, unexpectedly, were found to oversail the rectangular Norman foundations. The four complex piers soar up to pointed arches at the same height as the nave and choir vaults,

Fig. 75 *The central tower seen from the south. In spite of being drastically scaled in the 18th century, rebuilt in the 19th and lacking its pinnacles along the balustrade, it has retained its original proportions and remains a splendid monument, dominating the landscape for many miles around.*

Fig. 76 *The interior of the central stage of the tower showing the large openings, now blocked.*

which give an extraordinary unity to the interior, unbroken except by Scott's lacy screen which serves only to mark the break between the western and eastern halves of the church — nave and crossing; choir and lady chapel.

The tracery of the upper part of the tower is Decorated, of the lower Perpendicular, a curious anomaly not easily explained. The central part of the tower originally may have been intended to be open, without a vault, forming a lofty lantern which would have made the crossing extraordinarily light and airy, but this seems to have been abandoned at an early stage, and the present vault inserted. The use of a tall open arcade to form the inner wall of the central stage of the tower may merely have been as a desire to reduce the weight of the structure.

At some time after the construction of the nave arcades, flying buttresses were inserted into the two eastern bays next to the tower, presumably because of some fears of, or actual, movement of the tower. The two buttresses are not identical, and may have been inserted at different times. That they were not built with the arcades is shown by the straight joints in the work and the slight differences in the stone (figs. 78 and 79).

Fig. 77 (Left) The crossing, showing the tierceron vault under the tower with elegant cusped decoration at its centre. The whitening of the compartments is recent and enhances the pattern of the ribs. It would almost certainly have been whitened originally and perhaps decorated with paintings.

Fig. 78 The flying buttresses inserted into the north arcade triforium and clerestory to support the tower pier seen to the right.

Fig. 79 The flying buttresses inserted into the south arcade triforium and clerestorey to support the tower pier seen to the left. Subsequently, due presumably to further problems of stability, the thicker curved buttress was inserted into the triforium of the second bay.

Since the four original buttresses appear to be contemporary, they are all later than the completion of both arcades c.1377. Note that while the triforia of both arcades are similar the clerestory of the later south arcade has triangular arches in contrast to the four-centred arches of the northern clerestory.

The Guesten Hall

The Guesten Hall was a five-bay ground floor hall, built in *c.*1320, with some of the most elaborate Decorated windows with flowing tracery in the whole cathedral complex (fig. 81). It had a splendid eight-bay roof with tiers of cusped and curved windbraces, dated 1326 — 'the most elegant of medieval carpentry in the county' (Pevsner, 1968, p.322). When the Guesten Hall was demolished in 1862 because money could not be found to save it, happily the roof was kept, modified and used on Holy Trinity church at Shrub Hill. When that church in turn was demolished the roof was preserved, and taken to the Avoncroft Museum of Buildings, near Bromsgrove, where it is now displayed over a new substructure (fig. 83).

Fig. 80 An engraving of the Guesten Hall made in the year before it was demolished. The porch with its upper door is already in ruins. Note also the ruined building joining the hall to thechapter house. (From the Hore collection)

Fig. 81 Internal elevation of the Guesten Hall. Compare with the same view photographed in 2000 (fig. 82). Note that the doorway is round-headed, not pointed as in the engraving and that a later inserted door has been blocked. (From the Hore collection)

Fig. 82 The east wall of the Guesten Hall, all that now remains. It dates from c.1320 with what must have been fine flowing tracery in the windows. The two left-hand windows end high up in the wall, because there was a building behind, perhaps a kitchen. There was also a prior's lodging beyond. Fig. 83 (below) The arched braced roof of the Guesten Hall as rebuilt at the Avoncroft Museum of Buildings at Bromsgrove.

Fig. 84 The east range of the cloister with the chapter house beyond.

The Cloister Vaults

The cloister was rebuilt in the 14th and 15th centuries, beginning with the east walk. The doorway from the church at the north-east corner is *c*.1300 while that at the north-west corner is Perpendicular. The vault has central octagons of lierne ribs, though the west walk differs in its details. The most striking feature is the rich variety of bosses in all the walks. In the east walk they are small, mostly of leaves and heads, but the south walk has the finest bosses, of figures and scenes culminating in the centre with the Coronation of the Virgin. The west walk has leaf bosses, while the north walk has applied figures of angels (fig. 86). It is possible that this walk was vaulted last, because of the new work in the south aisle of the church. It is not clear how much of this vaulting was painted though it is very probable that the bosses and figures were polychrome, and the severies, or compartments, white-washed to give greater light. This is not now obvious, though detailed examination may determine whether any colour has survived the weathering of the stone and the Victorian scraping. The four angels in the centre bay of the south walk do appear to retain traces of paint as do some of the bosses in the west walk.

An 1866 description says: 'Some of the groinings which are of a different coloured stone, are very fine, and a few in Bath stone … appear almost as perfect as if they were carved a twelve months ago … some are so dilapidated as to be indistinguishable. The best (preserved) appear to be in Caen stone, or in some limestone closely resembling it. Those which have crumbled away are in Highley sandstone (New Red) or in North Cotswold Öolite, which is of variable quality'. In other words, the varied state of preservation is due to the variety of stones used in the cloister vaults (fig. 87).

The window tracery throughout is by Perkins, who replaced tracery of the 18th century.

Fig. 85 The lierne vault of the south walk of the cloister.

Fig. 86 The lierne vault of the north walk of the cloister with many angels carrying shields. The date is perhaps c.1377, the date of the nave vault.

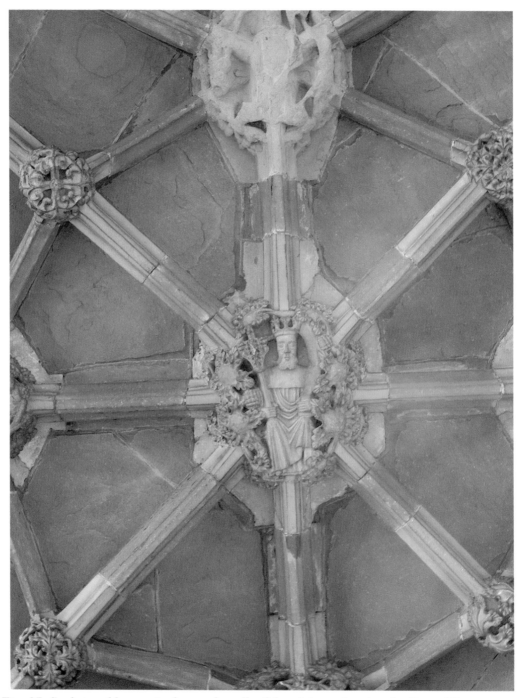

Fig. 87 Sculptured bosses in the south walk of the cloister showing the Tree of Jesse.
Notice the remarkable preservation of all but one of these sculptures, due to the stone used.
The boss at the top, probably of Highley stone, has almost eroded away, while the others,
perhaps of Caen stone, are nearly perfect and show varied discolouration which may be
the remains of paint.

69

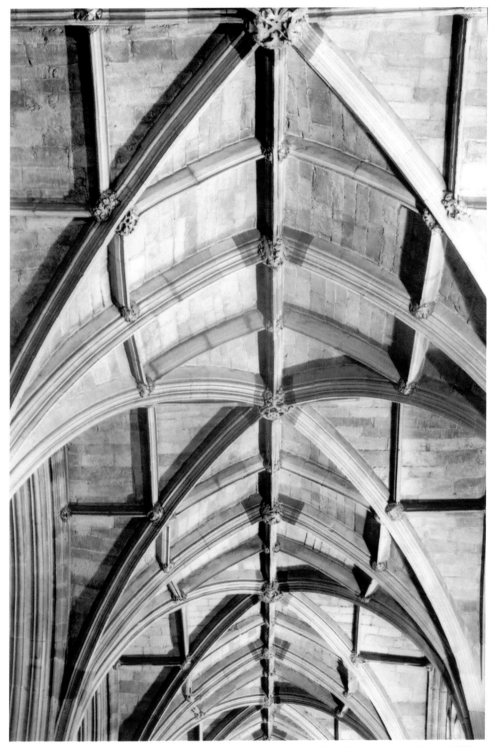

Fig. 88   The lierne vault of the south aisle of the nave, probably dating from about 1377, the date of the nave vault.

Fig. 89 The monastic refectory (College Hall) seen from College Green. Note the undercroft with a 12th-century door to the right (the pointed arched doorway on the left is 19th century). The hall above was considerably modified in the 14th century, with large Decorated windows, heavily restored in the 19th century.

Fig. 90 The exterior of the chapter house, seen from the south-east. The upper walls have been cut back to make them thinner, and the large windows, with Perpendicular tracery, inserted replacing the original smaller Norman windows. The lower walls have also been cut back, only less so, and the buttresses and parapet added transforming the exterior from Norman to Perpendicular.

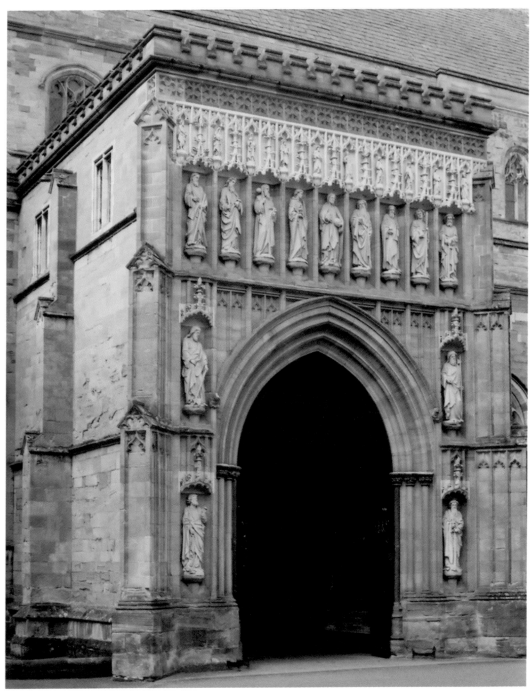

Fig. 91 The north porch. This 14th-century porch may have replaced a porch, probably of the same size, of Wulfstan's time. Wulfstan's porch, like that still existing at Tewkesbury, may have been barrel-vaulted. The whole front of this porch was taken down and rebuilt in the 19th-century restoration and the statues all date from that time. There are rooms above the porch, now used by the cathedral archaeologist.

Fig. 92 The east wall of the north-west transept showing the original Norman arch into a side chapel, (now destroyed) and the 14th-century arch which replaced its pair into the choir aisle. Above, the wall has been transformed into the Perpendicular style by the addition of panelling, Perpendicular windows, and a decorative quatrefoil parapet under the clerestory.

Fig. 93 The painted decoration of the 14th-century arch into the north choir aisle, consisting of rosettes and painted zigzag ornament reminiscent of Romanesque ornament. Between the attached shafts below can be seen the ghost of a crocketed canopy.

WORCESTER CATHEDRAL
SOUTH-WEST TRANSEPT

EXTERNAL ELEVATION   WEST FACE

Client:

The Sarum Partnership
on Behalf of
the Dean and Chapter of Worcester

scale: 0 ___ 1m
date: May/June 1992
drawn: DMA, PPB, PJS
traced: PAWS

STRATASCAN
Tiltridge Farm
Upton-upon-Severn
Tel: (0684) 592266
FAX: (0684) 594142

Fig. 94 (Above) Stone by stone drawing of the west face of the south-west transept.

Fig. 95 (Right) Interpretation of figure 94.

WORCESTER CATHEDRAL
SOUTH-WEST TRANSEPT
EXTERNAL ELEVATION   WEST FACE

The Water Gate

The present Water Gate dates from 1378, and excavations there in 1993 suggested that it is the first structure on the site, though the Severn has undoubtedly been used for river traffic since Roman times, if not before, and there is some evidence of an early crossing-point here. Until the mid-19th century the

Fig. 96 The Water Gate from the river, which is in flood, showing the depth of water which may have filled the gate at high tide. The conjectural outline of the upper storey housing the portcullis machinery has been superimposed on the present house.

river was tidal, so the Water Gate would flood twice a day, forming a small dock into which boats could be brought for unloading.

A ground-probing radar survey carried out on the landward side of the gate on the road which slopes up to College Green appears to confirm the suggestion that there was a slipway up which boats could be hauled through the gate and up the slope, probably by means of a winch. Excavation here might confirm this.

The gate has two archways, the inner rebated for a pair of doors, with their hinges still in place; the outer with a portcullis slot that continues 1.1m (3ft 6ins) below the present road level. This portcullis slot implies that there was a building above the gate, presumably also of sandstone and probably crenellated, tall enough to house both the portcullis when it was lifted and the winch necessary to lift it (fig. 96).

The gate is at least as defensible as the Edgar Tower, the gateway from the city into the precinct, and suggests that the precinct was felt to be more vulnerable from this side, or perhaps that valuable cargoes needed protection — these were the years of the Peasants' Revolt.

Excavation has shown that the southern wall which extends from the gate towards the river is 2.4m (7ft 10ins) deep at the towpath end, and has not only graffiti below present ground level but iron rings for tying up boats. This wall, which appears at first sight to be Victorian, must be earlier than the creation of the towpath on this side of the river. Pictorial evidence suggests that this was before 1823, so that the wall is probably late 18th century in date.

The inner walls of the gateway have a mass of graffiti on both sides (though unfortunately no dates) among them the life-size outline of a salmon, caught here in perhaps 1813 or, more probably, in the 1840s.

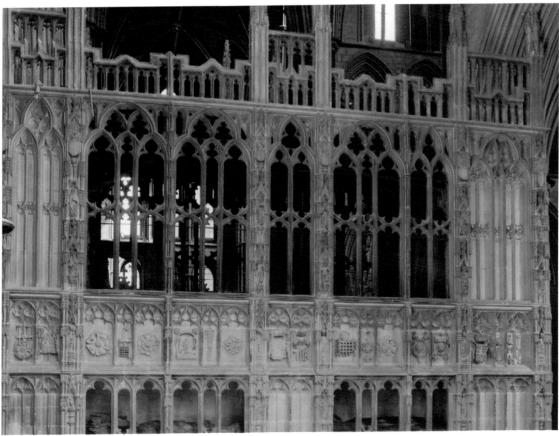

Fig. 97 On the south side the chantry is lower than on the north and incorporates two earlier, perhaps late 13th- to early 14th-century, monuments possibly to members of the Giffard family, seen at the bottom of the photograph.

Prince Arthur's Chantry

Prince Arthur, eldest son of Henry VII, died at Ludlow in 1502 and is buried in a magnificently carved chantry chapel south of the high altar. The construction of the chapel was not started until 1504 and seems not to have been finished for at least 12 years. Incorporated into the base of the chantry are tombs said to be of Bishop Giffard (d.1302) and his sister Matilda d'Evreux (d.1297). Above these tombs there is a band of Tudor iconography, in a different stone to the rest of the chantry, which appears to have been inserted. It is possible that the whole chantry is an adaptation of Giffard's own monument, which he had built before

his death. Such alterations might explain the damage to the pinnacles and the adjacent arcades.

The decoration of the chantry may not have been completed. Although the central panel of the reredos, depicting Christ as the Man of Sorrows, still retains its polychromy, it is probable that other sculptures should have been painted. In particular the blank shields supported by angels on the north and south sides of the chantry would have had coats of arms painted on them.

A detailed survey of the Chantry, including a ground-penetrating radar survey of the floor and tomb chest, was carried out in 2001-02. A

Fig. 98 The interior of Prince Arthur's chantry showing the lierne vault with pendants, and the wonderfully elaborate reredos with the Christ as the Man of Sorrows at its centre, carved flat after the Reformation so that it could be covered with painted plaster.

Fig. 99 (Left) Prince Arthur's chantry is built in the late Perpendicular style with much openwork, including the decorative crenellation. There are many heraldic symbols and figures of angels, saints, kings and bishops in canopies.

conference was held in May 2002 to mark the 500th anniversary of Prince Arthur's death and the papers presented will be published.

8. DECAY AND RESTORATION FROM THE 16TH TO THE 19TH CENTURIES

At the dissolution of the priory, in 1539, many of the minor monastic buildings were converted into houses for the new prebendaries and canons and other ministers of the new foundation, but the greater monastic buildings probably survived unaltered until the Civil War.

On the Feast of the Assumption in 1537, the Shrine of Our Lady of Worcester had been despoiled and her jewels, coat and shoes had been taken away.

In 1538 the shrines of St Oswald and St Wulfstan were taken down and their relics buried at the north end of the high altar (it is said wrapped in lead with the bones of Bishop Constantiis). An excavation there in 1971 failed to find them.

On 10 January 1547 'Images were destroyed over the whole church.' The usual practice seems to have been to destroy completely statues that were within easy reach, or to knock off their heads. Others more inaccessible often survived. By and large, only those statues considered idolatrous, such as those of Christ, the Virgin Mary and the saints were attacked. The fine sculptures in the spandrels of the eastern transepts and the misericords, for example, were left untouched.

In 1551 the choir was moved from its position two bays west of the crossing to its present position. At the same time a platform which extended under the crossing and into the eastern two bays of the nave was removed.

The Civil War brought considerably more destruction to the cathedral and its monastic buildings. On Saturday 24 September 1642 the Parliamentary troops under the Earl of Essex entered Worcester as an occupying army and on the next day, Sunday 25, an orgy of desecration and destruction began in the cathedral. Service books, vestments, windows and statues were destroyed, horses were stabled in the nave and cloisters and camp fires lit, and the choir and aisles were used as latrines. The occupation only lasted a little over a month, but the damage done to the building and its furniture is incalculable.

In July 1646 Worcester again fell to the Parliamentarians after a long siege and in 1647 it was decided that a 'leaden steeple in the Cathedral Churchyard' then used as a woodhouse 'should be stripped of its lead, which should be sold for the re-edification and repair of Almshouses and churches'. This steeple was, without doubt, the detached bell tower which stood close to the cathedral on the north-east side. Probably at about the same time, roof timbers and lead were stripped from the east transept with its lead pinnacle, the vestries or south chapels of the choir, the chapter house, the dormitory, the cloister, and the gate house (presumably the Edgar Tower). At the same time the lead conduit pipe which brought water from Henwick Road to the lavatorium in the cloister, a pipe no less than 2,140 yards long, was removed and the conduit houses and a lead cistern destroyed.

The document drawn up by Canon Barnabas Oley which lists this destruction is dated 6 November 1660, soon after the Restoration of the Monarchy, and suggests that it was made in preparation for repairing the cathedral and

Fig. 100 The nave (from Wild 1823) showing the Perpendicular stone screen with organ above which blocked off the choir and chancel until Perkins and Scott opened up the vista in their reorganisation of the interior.

the major buildings at least, since they would rapidly deteriorate without their roofs.

There is also evidence that it was at this time that Charles II restored the cathedral rents in order to provide money for the repairs and upkeep of the cathedral and its ancilliary buildings.

Major repairs were carried out from 1712-1715 when £7,000 was spent, an enormous amount at that time. The outer walls were cased and the pinnacles at the corners of the central tower were rebuilt, while the interior was strengthened with inserted walls and arches.

The tall spires, which are shown on engravings of that date (fig. 101), but not

on Dugdale's view of 1672, must have been added at about that time.

The sacrist's lodging, which was built outside the west end of the north choir aisle, was taken down, but the oriel window, inside the church, which gave the sacrist a view into the interior from his house, can still be seen (fig. 102).

Another major campaign of repairs, which lasted for eight years, was carried out between 1748 and 1756 when the north end of the north transept was rebuilt. The great flying buttresses at the east end were built between 1736 and 1789 (fig. 101), while the window at the west end was rebuilt in 1789 and that at the east end in 1792 (fig. 103).

Fig. 101   The cathedral (from Wild 1823) seen from the north-east showing the tall pinnacles and flying buttresses removed by Perkins together with the Decorated style east window of 1792.

The great tower was scaled several inches deep at about this time, by which, as Willis says, 'its architectural character was greatly injured'. A new altar screen and a new choir screen were set up in 1812; the tall pinnacles were taken down some time after 1832, and, finally, in 1857, the major restoration was begun under the direction of Abraham Perkins, the cathedral architect, who had the foresight to leave a part of the cathedral (in the north choir aisle) untouched, to show succeeding generations, including us, the state of the building as he found it, weathered and broken and covered with whitewash, (fig. 106). Whatever our opinion of the drastic Victorian restoration, the cathedral could not have been left as it was, run down and patched up with temporary expedients. As Willis says 'in the interior, settlement of the piers and arches in the Early English work [that is the lady chapel and choir] had attained so alarming a magnitude as to threaten the stability of the structure.' And the walls and arches inserted in 1712 were themselves giving way 'having

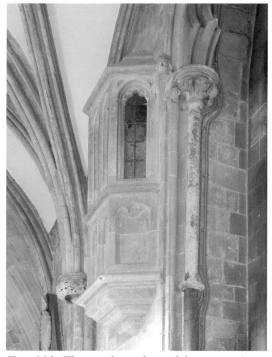

Fig. 102 The oriel window of the sacrist's lodging, seen inside the north choir aisle. From here the sacrist could keep his eye on the high altar and the sanctuary.

L   Old west window. Erected 1380
M   New Window. Erected 1789

J   Ancient east window
K   New Window. Erected 1792

Fig. 103 Showing the old east and west windows and their 18th-century replacements which were swept away in the 19th-century restoration. (From Valentine Green, Worcester, *Vol.I (1796)).*

Fig. 104 The east end of the cathedral (from Wild 1823) with King John's tomb in the foreground, showing the 18th-century east window (seen from outside in fig. 101) and the screen behind the high altar (also seen in fig. 107, which was engraved in 1863, after the east window had been altered, but before the new reredos was built in 1877).

Fig. 105 The choir in a print by Wild of 1823 showing the 18th-century choir stalls with their elaborate wooden colonnades and the great organ above the screen. The medieval choir stalls seem to have been swept away, though the misericords, which still exist in their original positions, must have been incorporated. The pulpit on the right dates from 1642.

served rather to change the direction of the settlements than to stop them' while an article on Worcester in *The Analyst*, Vol. ii, p.98, 1835 begins 'perhaps no English Cathedral presents so heterogeneous an appearance, in its external aspect, such a patched and thread-bare coat of many colours, presenting so little to admire, and so much to deplore as the Cathedral at Worcester.'

9. THE VICTORIAN RESTORATION

In spite of large sums spent on the cathedral between 1818 and 1834, when expenditure only fell below £500 twice and was often nearer £1,000, Thomas Rickman wrote in 1833 'I find the music meeting is to be held in the Cathedral now though I do not say the roof will fall I do say that I think it dangerous to have the music meeting there with the Groining in the state it is nor would I myself go to the Cathedral on the occasion.'

But such awful possibilities are belied by Charles Wild's contemporary view of the nave where the triennial music festivals were held (see fig. 100).

Sir Robert Smirke, consulted in the same year, thought that the chief problem was with the structure of the main roofs, where the timbers had parted company with the walls, but that if these roofs could be repaired, a small permanent workforce could deal with the other problems of the fabric. By 1845 a local architect, Abraham Perkins, had become cathedral architect and he began the general restoration in 1857. He was joined by George

Fig. 106 Two tombs in the north choir aisle, deliberately omitted from the Victorian reconstruction to show the state of the cathedral as Perkins and Scott found it — broken and eroded and covered with whitewash.

(later Sir George) Gilbert Scott in 1864. It is these two men together with the Ecclesiastical Commissioners' architect, Ewan Christian, who were responsible for the drastic alterations, amounting in some cases to complete rebuilding, which give the cathedral much of the character it now has. This character is not being altered by the present restoration which is being carried out on entirely different principles (see chapter 11).

Perkins removed many late medieval, 17th- and 18th-century features, including window tracery, screens, buttresses and pinnacles, completely demolished and rebuilt a large proportion of the east end, and took down much of the central tower and remodelled it. Most of this restoration and renewal was due to the condition of the fabric, which had suffered from the fact that in the past a great deal of vulnerable, easily weathered stone had been used. Many inappropriate piecemeal additions were properly swept away, but at the same time, there was a continuous, and sometimes acrimonious debate, not on the structural solutions to be adopted, but on the architectural styles which should be used in the areas of rebuilding. It is interesting to see that attitudes towards late medieval, 17th- and 18th-century work changed during the course of the restoration, but in general most post-medieval work was considered 'bad'.

Fig. 107 The lady chapel in 1863 after the insertion of Perkins' new 'Early English' windows but before the screen was replaced by the present reredos in 1877. (Engraving in The Builder *1863).*

Fig. 108 The east end with Perkins' east windows on the left and much original 13th-century work on the right. The stained glass is by Hardman.

For example, in 1853-54 the Ecclesiastical Commissioners asked Ewan Christian to report on the fabric. While he thought that 'the main features of the architecture are in all parts still clearly distinguishable and especially in the earlier portion are extremely beautiful' he nevertheless wrote that three windows of the choir clerestory 'have been filled with course [sic] tracery executed in Higley [sic] stone and are in every respect of the worst possible character ...'. However, Perkins had already gone ahead and begun to replace them to match the original Early English work still remaining at the east end.

In 1855-56 Perkins restored the lady chapel and demolished the south-east transept flying buttresses. It is typical of the confusion and disagreement surrounding much of the restoration that Ewan Christian thought that the buttresses were 'not later than the mid-fifteenth century'; Britton, who engraved views of the cathedral, thought they were 15th century; Willis thought (after their demolition) that they had been 18th century, while Perkins himself calls them 'added'. However, since in 1686 some £200 was bequeathed towards buttresses to the choir and lady chapel, they may, in fact, have been 17th century.

While Christian's report is silent on the question of the great east window, Perkins takes the opportunity of suggesting in a pencilled note on the report 'If the eastern gable be taken down [as Christian had agreed] won't it be advisable to replace the large window by a five-light lancet [i.e. Early English] window — which — or something similar — was probably there before the present ugly one?'

Fig. 109 The chancel with the high altar and the reredos. This illustrates clearly the unity achieved by Perkins and Scott, merging their new work with the existing 13th-century building.

Fig. 110 The north side of the choir. Compare with fig. 105, a print dating from 1823. The screens, the canopies, the organ and the choir stalls are all by Scott, though the back rows of the choir stalls on each side contain a fine series of misericords of 1379.

Fig. 111 The choir screen, by Scott. This open work screen which replaced the stone screen of the 14th- or 15th-century seen in fig. 100, enables the building to be seen as a whole from east or west instead of divided into separate spaces. As Pevsner says 'the greatest asset of Worcester is the unity of its interior'.

The assumption was that the east and west windows were both late 18th century and therefore despicable. A cathedral guide of 1854 describes the tracery and glass of the new east window erected in 1789 as 'very bad'. Informed opinion was clearly on Perkins' side and he rebuilt the east end accordingly and both Willis and Christian recorded their approval, Christian reporting that 'the effect of the building in its restored state is exceedingly beautiful'.

However, by 1862 opinion regarding the wholesale replacement of ancient windows and other features with modern copies of earlier styles was beginning to change and Willis himself gave his view that there was no historical justification for an Early English window at one end of the great transept and a Decorated window at the other. Fortunately for Perkins, criticism was deflected by the controversy over the demolition of the Guesten Hall in that year.

Between 1863 and 1865 the new west window and door were built. The lower part of the west door is late 12th-century and can be distinguished from the 19th-century work

Fig. 112 The east end of the cathedral seen from the south with the south-eastern transept on the right. This shows the way in which Perkins married his new work with the original Early English east end, since only the clerestory is medieval.

by the character of the tooling, while below the 12th-century bases the 11th-century bases still remain *in situ* (fig. 53). Fig. 103 shows the successive 14th-century and 18th-century windows which were replaced by Perkins' geometrical Decorated window.

In 1866 opinion had changed sufficiently for the *Saturday Review* to attack the work being done at Worcester: 'What then do we find this Dean and Chapter doing? They are letting loose a local genius to work his will upon the venerable walls, which other and better men have raised, and the form of which they themselves could never have distantly approached in conception …'.

As early as 1850 George Gilbert Scott had written 'an authentic feature, though late and poor, is more worthy than an earlier though fine part conjecturally restored — a plain fact,

than ornamental conjuncture'. By 1862 Scott was arguing for 'conservative' restoration — the philosophy of the present day.

In the case of Worcester, Perkins' views prevailed and a great deal of his restoration consisted, as we have seen, of rebuilding in close imitation of earlier medieval styles.

After 1864 the major restoration was that of the tower which was strengthened in the hope that it would 'have the finest peal of bells in the country'. The outer walls were taken down perhaps as far as the main roofs, and the plans of the walls laid out on the floor of the cathedral nave before the rebuilding.

While the style of the tower was generally retained, early engravings and other evidence show that a number of details were altered, in particular, the silhouette was changed by the addition of 2 feet to the height of the parapet

Fig. 113 The great west window, 1863-65.

Fig. 114 Victorian splendour. The reredos, designed by Scott and made by Farmer and Brindley.

(which had small finials, now removed) and 7 feet to the height of the pinnacles.

The front wall of the north porch was taken down and rebuilt in 1865 and Hardman and Forsyth supplied a complete new sculptural scheme. The ground outside the north side of the cathedral was lowered at this time — the raised pavement outside the houses of College Yard shows by how much — and the cloister garth was lowered by 0.5m (1.5 feet).

In 1868 the structural restoration was complete, and Scott began the reorganisation of the interior (see figs. 110 and 111). He designed the sumptuous reredos and the screens, including the open screen in the style of the 13th century; the choir stalls (which, however, incorporate the marvellous series

of misericords of 1379) and the choir organ cases. The nave pulpit, in the Italian style, was designed by Scott and carved by Forsyth. The stained glass throughout is 19th century, and will be the subject of a separate book, as will the very varied sculpture in the cathedral.

The restoration was virtually complete by 1874, and the achievement was celebrated by a round of re-opening ceremonies, the first attended by some 3,000 people, many of whom processed through the city with flags and banners. £114,295 11s 4d had been spent since 1840 and this huge sum, similar in its day to the amount being spent on the present restoration, put Worcester at the top of the restoration 'league table' published in *The Builder* in 1876.

Fig. 115 The back of the reredos, sumptuously decorated, the alabaster incised and painted in red and gold with a cross and the symbols of the Evangelists. Dedicated to Dean Peel and his wife, 1877.

Fig. 116 Plan of excavations adjacent to the exterior of the chapter house.

10.   THE CHAPTER HOUSE EXCAVATIONS

Archaeological work outside the Chapter House in the 1990s revealed a curving wall, concentric with the Chapter House and 3 metres from it. This wall has a mortared rubble foundation up to 1.5 metres wide and at least 0.75 metres deep. In places the rubble core and sandstone facing blocks forming the lowest course or two of the wall itself, which was 1 metre wide, survive.

Projecting out from beneath the 14th-century buttresses of the present building are the foundations of sleeper walls, also of mortared rubble, which are of one build with the curving wall. On the outer face of the curving wall opposite these sleeper walls are narrow pilaster buttresses set on the offset foundations.

In places, beneath the remodelled Chapter House walls, the outer edge of an earlier curving foundation has been observed, presumably that of the Romanesque Chapter House constructed in the early 12th century. Unfortunately it has not been possible to establish a direct link between these foundations and the sleeper walls and the curving wall because the junctions underlie the 14th-century buttresses.

It is the function and date of the outer wall and the associated sleeper walls which are of the greatest importance. It is clear from the excavations that they are pre-14th century in date, since they underlie the buttresses of that date and the curving wall was partly robbed out at that time. Although it is possible that they form the remains of an ambulatory around the outside of the Norman Chapter House, such as a structure would be unique and of no purpose, since it would seem to lead from and back to the cloister and there is no evidence that it could be accessed directly from the Chapter House.

Another possibility considered is that these walls formed part of a round building predating the Norman Chapter House, the central core of which would have been where the present building is. The sleeper walls may have supported piers forming an arcade while there may have been additional piers to support the roof of the central portion.

In 2003 excavations were carried out inside the Chapter House in advance of the installation of under-floor heating and a new stone floor. These provided an opportunity to test the hypotheses presented above and also to find out more about the central pillar (see the section on the Chapter House in Chapter 3 above).

The excavations showed that the foundations of the Chapter House are composed of layers of slag between bands of mortar, like those of the west end of the Crypt and not like those of the outer curving wall. There was also no evidence to show that the sleeper walls had continued into the area occupied by the present building or that there had been arcade piers with the spaces between them infilled. It is therefore clear that the outer curving wall and the associated sleeper walls are later than the Norman Chapter House, not earlier, although their function is still uncertain.

The excavation did however show that the base of the central column had been replaced in the 13th century. The original stone foundation of the column was sealed by a layer of soil which was cut by mortar abutting the new base. There were also several post-holes

Fig. 117 View from above of excavations adjacent to the south side of the chapter house. Note the curving wall.

around the central pillar, showing that the vault had been supported while the pillar base was renewed.

The major result of the excavation was the discovery of an Anglo-Saxon Christian cemetery below the Chapter House. About 180 burials were excavated while many more were left in place. The skeletons were those of men, women and children and thus represent the general population of Worcester, not monks. Many of the burials were in wooden coffins and in some cases stones had been placed around the head of the deceased. There were also some instances of textiles surviving, presumably the remains of woollen shrouds.

The majority of the burials have been dated to the Anglo-Saxon period because, as mentioned above, they include women and children and also because some of the burials are cut by the foundations of the building. In some cases only the base of the coffin or part of the skeleton survived because the rest of the burial had been removed by the insertion of later floors in the Chapter House. There were, however, at least two medieval burials. The first was just inside the Norman doorway and the grave was lined with mortar and had a shaped recess to the head. The skeleton only partly survived because of later disturbance but had been buried in s shroud. The second burial was in a stone-lined cist between the first and the central pillar. Again only part of the skeleton remained undisturbed but it was that of a man 5'8" tall and aged 50+. He had been buried wearing a pair of leather boots and these have been dated to the period 1370-1420. The burials have yet to be fully analysed but could provide much information on the population of Worcester before the Norman Conquest.

11.   THE PRESENT RESTORATION

Great buildings such as the cathedral seem to require major restoration about once every century. The situation at Worcester is compounded because much of the local stone used over the centuries was soft and friable and eroded very quickly: see for example the exterior of the two western bays on the north side which have lost all their detail (fig. 52). The stone used in the Victorian restoration appears to have deteriorated more rapidly, exacerbated by widespread use of ironwork in cramps, tie bars, rods, shims and bands which expands dramatically when it corrodes, causing great damage to the stonework.

During the 20th century the two World Wars and the depression of the 1930s made extensive restoration programmes out of the question. After 1945 isolated repairs were undertaken to the cathedral, the major element of which was to the masonry of the tower in about 1950. The following decades saw the recovering of the lead roof to the nave north aisle, north porch and Jesus chapel and re-leading of the south nave aisle above the library in 1981.

During the mid-1970s the then cathedral architect, Bernard Ashwell, became aware of failing masonry to the four main piers which

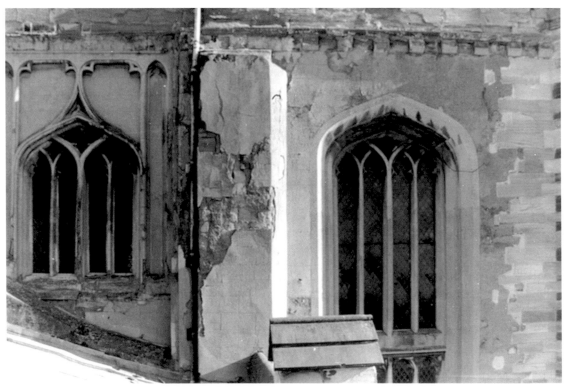

Fig. 118 The west face of the south-west transept showing the condition of the rendering and masonry before repair. (Photograph by Helen Lubin)

support the central tower. Stones were spalling at an increasing rate and Mr Ashwell became suspicious that the facing stones to the piers were becoming over-stressed. Various investigations were carried out including drilling into the core of the piers in several places, radar surveys and other means. It was essential to ascertain whether the foundations of the piers were sound or whether they were the cause of the problem and excavations were made to each pier in turn in 1981, 1983, 1985 and 1987. As a result of all these investigations, it was ascertained that the medieval core of the piers, which was made up of broken stone, rubble and mortar at the time of the construction, had settled leaving numerous large voids. As a result the weight of the tower above, thought to be approximately 5,000 tonnes, was being taken by the thin outer facing of the piers resulting in stresses beyond the strength of the stones with consequential spalling and failures. It was calculated that the failures would accelerate and that if no action was taken the tower was more than likely to collapse by the year 2000.

Fig. 119 The north-west nave aisle buttress showing the disintegration of the stone.

Mr Ashwell retired in 1985 and was succeeded by Mr Kenneth Wiltshire who undertook a very detailed inspection and survey of the entire cathedral fabric. This report identified not only the very dangerous state of the tower but also the poor condition of the high-level roofs as well as the enormous scale of stone decay to the cathedral exterior.

A major appeal was launched in 1988 which was successful and this allowed the repairs to the tower to proceed quickly.

The area around the tower was totally screened off for a year, during which time the cathedral celebrated major services with the altar at the west end of the nave. More than 1,400 holes were drilled into the piers to receive stainless steel bars which penetrated deep into the core. These were grouted at the same time. This process tied the pier facings back to the core to provide a homogenous load-bearing structure. At the same time a concrete ring beam was inserted within the thickness of the tower walls at the clock floor level to give additional stability. During these investigations and works some very interesting discoveries were made. The first was the presence of a headless burial by the base of the south-east pier. He has now become known as the Worcester pilgrim and his staff and his leather boots which survived have now been put on display in the crypt. The second discovery was that on the east side evidence was found suggesting that there may have been a panic in the 13th century when masons were carrying out alterations to the choir. Movement had clearly taken place during the course of the work and the Norman triforium gallery was not entirely taken down where it abutted the tower and had been very hastily filled leaving a certain number of voids. Similar evidence of rapid buttressing was also found in the crypt area when the new entrance steps had been formed earlier (see chapters 3 and 6).

Although the public appeal had been very successful the Dean and Chapter were aware that the entire repair programme identified by Mr Wiltshire in 1986 would cost at least £10 million. Of the original sum raised by the appeal over £2 million was retained and invested to provide a continuing income. This income together with successful applications to English Heritage for grant aid under the then new cathedral grants scheme enabled the Dean and Chapter to plan a 15 to 20 year repair programme.

An essential pre-requisite of the repair programme was the erection of new workshops to the south of the lady chapel and the training and appointment of new stone masons to work on the stone repairs.

The main high-level roofs, all of which are covered with Welsh slate with lead parapet gutters, were re-laid re-using as many of the salvaged slates as possible, supplemented by new Penrhyn slate to replace decayed or broken slates. Lead parapets were re-laid with new lead with shorter bays to give a longer life to the leadwork. The opportunity was also taken to install smoke vents to the roof voids which would allow the release of hot gases which would rise in the event of a fire within the roof spaces. The fire at York Minster in 1986 identified the need to dissipate the hot products of combustion quickly.

The original timber roof structure was retained as much as possible but in some cases, particularly to the roof timbers of the nave, decay in the main trusses was so great that strengthening with steel work was necessary.

The other essential part of the repair programme was the repair of the external stonework which was acknowledged by English Heritage as probably being in the worst state of any of the English cathedrals.

The stonework is nearly all sandstone from the Severn valley but Victorian restoration work in the east end of the cathedral intro-

Fig. 120 The nave roof showing the rotted foot of one of the principal trusses.

duced some limestone to pinnacles, window surrounds, buttresses and so on. Sandstones used throughout the cathedral are calcerious, that is that they react with lime and the water run-off from the Victorian limestone has caused considerable decay of adjacent sandstone. The widespread use of ironwork with consequential problems of corrosion has already been referred to.

A long programme of stonework repairs was started beginning at the west end of the cathedral and then moving to the east end. Wherever possible all stones are retained except where the degree of decay is so great that a stone will not survive until the next restoration. Unfortunately, sandstone does not react positively to many of the conservation techniques which are applied successfully to limestone.

A long programme of stonework repairs was started beginning at the west end of the cathedral and then moving to the east end. Wherever possible all stones are retained except where the degree of decay is so great that a stone will not survive until the next restoration. Unfortunately, sandstone does not react positively to many of the conservation techniques which are applied successfully to limestone.

At the time of writing, all of the roofs have been recovered and work is currently underway to the cloister garth masonry, this being the last section of the original 1988 restoration programme. It will have taken exactly 20 years and cost £10 million, all as predicted by Mr Wiltshire in 1988. It should be noted that English Heritage has contributed more than £2.5 million towards this cost.

There have been considerable problems with pinnacles due mainly to the effect of corrosion of iron reinforcement which was much used in their construction. The corrosion was so serious that the pinnacles to the south-west and north-east transepts became dangerous and were taken down over the last 70 years. The two pinnacles to the north-east transept have been rebuilt by the cathedral's own masons, to a design similar to those on the south-east transept. The two remaining missing pinnacles, to the south-west transept, will be re-built as soon as funds permit. These will be larger and more substantial and will probably be constructed in a design similar

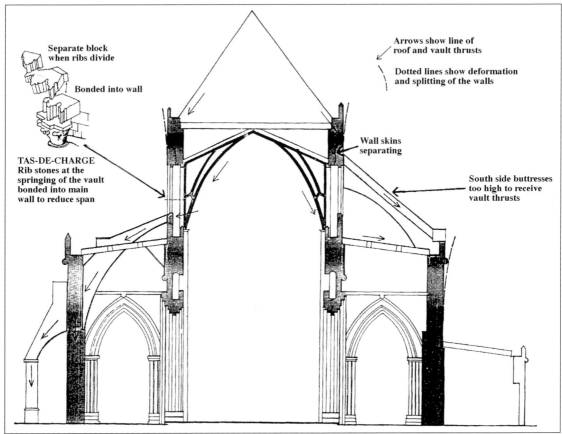

Fig. 121 Cross section through the cathedral showing some of the causes of the major potential structural failures which the present programme of repairs is designed to correct.

to those on the north-west transept, although unlike recently erected pinnacles, better photographs of the original ones survive. The stonework repairs to the cloister garth will also include first replacements of the 24 missing pinnacles in that quadrangle.

Upon completion of the original repair programme, repairs will continue to be carried out, on a reduced scale. The cathedral's own masons will continue to be kept in full time employment.

Completion of the external repair programme now enables the Chapter to concentrate on internal work. New organs are being provided in the choir and a further new instrument will be provided in the nave. The large organ case, currently in the south-west transept, will be modified and relocated in the north-west transept to give more natural daylight under the tower crossing. This large case provides space for the large 32-foot long pipes because there is insufficient room for inclusion in the new organ cases in the choir and the nave. Both instruments will share the use of these large pipes.

It is also hoped to clean the interior of the east end of the cathedral where centuries of accumulated dirt and smoke from old stoves has made the walls and ceilings particularly dirty.

New lighting is to be installed throughout the cathedral, not only to provide adequate lighting for the various activities, but also to enhance the architectural form of the Cathedral building whilst at the same time offering a considerable reduction in running costs.

Credit must be given to the long succession of architects, masons and carpenters who have worked on the cathedral, some of whose names, at least from the early 13th, are known. Among the most important are:

Alexander, *floruit* 1224-1257, who was responsible for the Early English lady chapel and perhaps the choir. He was master of the work at Lincoln Cathedral from about 1240;

William of Schokerwicke, master mason in 1316;

Nicholas de Obedone, carpenter, *fl.* 1351-1360;

John Clyve, fl. 1362-1392, the master mason responsible for the tower, the north porch, the east cloister, the recasing of the chapter house, the south arcade and the vault of the nave. John Harvey in *English Medieval Architects*, 1984, p.62, describes the tower and the north porch as 'among the masterpieces of English art';

The 'Master of the Earl of Warwick', *fl.* 1392 – (worked at Worcester);

Robert Kerver, *fl.* 1409-1410, was a carver who may have been responsible for the vault bosses of the cloister;

John Chapman, *fl.* 1435-1436, master of the masons, who was engaged on the west walk of the cloister.

Fig. 122 Map showing principal quarries which have supplied stone to the cathedral up to the present day.

12. The Building Stones used in the Cathedral

Both the interior and the exterior of the cathedral are constructed in stones from various sources. Only limited research has been undertaken into the origins of the stones—by Robert Willis in his 1863 *Architectural History of the Cathedral* and by Canon Wilson in a paper to the Worcester Archaeological Society in 1911.

Until recent times the supply of stone was limited by the transport available and not surprisingly most of the quarries which supplied the cathedral in early days were very close to the River Severn or its tributaries although some must have been transported over land from quarry to river (fig. 122). In Saxon times the stone would appear to have come principally from Alveley. This greyish-green stone is a Triassic sandstone and is found in numerous locations around the cathedral including the lower courses of the interior of the chapter house and also the nave arcade piers. Early supplies of stone also came from Holt, approximately six miles above Worcester up the River Severn.

Öolitic limestone was brought to the cathedral from early times from Guiting for the eastern slype whilst the limestone in the crypt is probably from Bredon, the quarry being close to the River Avon which joins the Severn at Tewkesbury. Some stones found in the chapter house are thought to come from further east, possibly Campden.

From the Norman period onwards stone came in large quantities from Highley, south of Bridgnorth. This greyish-green stone, sparsely speckled with mica and white spots indicating the presence of feldspar, is found in many locations including the two western bays of the nave, the chapter house walls and the tower staircase as well as elsewhere. Alveley and Holt sandstones continued to be used during the Norman period.

Towards the end of the Norman period, the 12th-century vaulting used a lightweight stone known as tufa. This is cream or white in colour and contains an abundance of casts of plant stems which gives it a very open texture. It is a calcareous limestone found mainly in the upper reaches of the River Teme from quarries at Shelsey, Stanford and Eastham. This stone is also found in various parts of Herefordshire although there is no evidence that any in the cathedral came from there.

The Early English work at the east end, started in 1224, uses much Öolitic limestone from several quarries in the north Cotswolds, including probably Bredon and Campden, but with shafts in Purbeck 'marble'. The Purbeck stone from Worth Matravers on the Purbeck peninsular in Dorset would have come by sea and river.

Holt red sandstone, which is an upper Triassic sandstone, is widely found in the 14th-century work. Limestone from Painswick was used around this time for the cloister floor and later for Prince Arthur's chantry.

There appear to be few records of stonework undertaken in the 17th and 18th centuries but in the 19th century it is known that stone from Hadley, near Ombersley, was widely used for facing the east end and the tower. In addition, the 19th-century work to the east end incorporates much Öolitic limestone which in view of improved transportation may well have come from more distant quarries such as Daglingworth near Cirencester, as well as those quarries which had supplied the cathedral earlier. Stone was also brought to the cathedral from Grinshall near Shrewsbury and Hollington in Staffordshire. It also appears that some beds of Highley stone were re-used in the 19th-century re-facing of the north-east transept.

The current restoration work has used stone from some existing sources but most are from new ones as the original quarries in many cases have long since closed or been worked out. Hollington continues to be used and whilst the mottled red-buff may appear odd there is evidence of such mottled stones being used earlier, in the 19th century. Lighter buff stone was obtained from Grinshill but of late a buff sandstone from a quarry near Halifax has been used which is a good match for the later beds of Highley used on the north-east transept. Grey-green stone from Barnhill, in the Forest of Dean, has also been used. Whilst this was a good colour match for the Highley on the north-west transept it is not such a good match for the north-east transept and the Halifax stone is better.

Some of the greener stones from Highley, particularly those to the bases of the nave arcades, have been replaced with a Glauconite sandstone from Hurdcott near Salisbury. Replacement for the limestone of the east end window surrounds and dressings comes from Limpley Stoke near Bath.

Research continues into finding replacement stones as it has been shown that even stones from the same quarries vary in their nature according to the beds used and when they were extracted.

GLOSSARY

ABACUS: The flat slab on the top of a capital (q.v.)

AMBULATORY: Semicircular or polygonal aisle enclosing an apse (q.v.)

APSE: Vaulted semicircular or polygonal end of a chancel or chapel

ARCADE: Range of arches supported on free-standing piers or columns,
        BLIND ARCADE, the same attached to a wall

ASHLAR: Masonry of large squared blocks

BAYS: Internal compartments of a building

BLOCK CAPITAL: Romanesque capital cut from a cube by having the lower angles rounded
        off to a circular shaft below (also called Cushion Capital)

CANOPY: Projection or hood over an altar, pulpit, niche, statue etc.

CAPITAL: The top part of a column, usually decorative

CHANCEL: The whole of the church east of the crossing excluding the lady chapel

CHANTRY CHAPEL: Chapel attached to, or inside, a church endowed for the saying of
        Masses for the soul of the founder

CHAMFER: Surface made by cutting the square edge of a block at an angle of 45°

CHEVRON: Norman moulding forming a zig-zag

CHOIR (QUIRE):   That part of the church where divine service is sung

CLERESTORY: Upper storey of the nave walls of a church, pierced by windows

CRENELLATION: Parapet with a series of embrasures with raised portions or merlons between

CROCKET: Decorative features placed on the sloping sides of spires, pinnacles, gables, etc. in
        Gothic architecture, carved in various leaf shapes and placed at regular intervals

CROCKET CAPITAL: An early Gothic form of stylised leaf shapes

CROSSING: The intersection of the nave, chancel and transepts

CRYPT: Underground room usually below the east end of the church

CUSHION CAPITAL   *see* Block Capital

CUSP: Projecting point between small arcs in Gothic tracery

DECORATED: Style of English Gothic architecture from *c.*1250 to *c.*1350

DOGTOOTH: Typical E.E. ornament consisting of four-cornered stars raised pyramidally

EARLY ENGLISH: (E.E) Historical division of English Gothic architecture roughly covering
        the 13th century

EMBRASURES: Regular openings in a parapet

ENGAGED COLUMNS: Columns attached to, or partly sunk into, a wall

FILLET: Narrow flat band running down a shaft or along a roll moulding (q.v.)

FINIAL: Top of a canopy, gable or pinnacle

GALLERY: In church architecture the upper storey above an aisle, opening in arches to the
        nave. Also called Tribune but often erroneously Triforium (q.v.)

GROIN: Sharp edge at the meeting of a cross-vault. Sometimes called an ARRIS

IMPOST: Bracket in a wall, usually formed of mouldings, on which the ends of an arch rest

JAMB: Straight side of an archway, doorway or window

LANCET WINDOW: Slender pointed-arched window

LANTERN: In architecture, a turret with windows all round crowning a roof or dome

LIERNE: *see* Vault

MISERICORD: Bracket on the underside of a hinged choir stall seat which, when lifted up, gave the occupant of the seat a support during long periods of standing (also called Miserere)

NAIL-HEAD: E.E. ornamental motif, consisting of regularly repeated small pyramids

PATERA: Small flat circular or oval ornament

PENDANT: Boss elongated so that it seems to hang down

PERPENDICULAR: Style of English Gothic architecture covering the period from *c.*1335-50 to *c.*1530

PIER: Strong, solid support, frequently square in section or of composite section (compound pier)

PILASTER: Shallow pier attached to a wall

PINNACLE: Ornamental form crowning a spire, tower, buttress, etc.

PLINTH: Projecting base of a wall or column, generally chamfered (q.v.) or moulded at the top

PRESBYTERY: The part of the church lying east of the choir containing the altar

PULPITUM: Stone screen in a major church provided to shut off the choir from the nave

QUOINS: Dressed stones at the angles of a building. Often they are alternately large and small

RADIATING CHAPELS: Chapels projecting radially from an ambulatory or an apse

REFECTORY: Dining hall

REREDOS: Structure behind and above an altar

RESPOND: Half-pier bonded into a wall and carrying one end of an arch

Fig. 123 One bay of the choir showing the terms used to describe its parts. (Drawn by Helen Lubin)

ROLL-MOULDING: Moulding of semicircular or more than semicircular section

ROMANESQUE: Style in architecture which was current in the 11th and 12th centuries and preceded the Gothic style (in England often called Norman)

ROOD: Cross or crucifix

SANCTUARY: Area around the main altar of a church

SCREEN: Parclose screen: screen separating a chapel from the rest of the church, ROOD SCREEN, screen below the rood, usually at the west end of a chancel

SEDILIA: Seats for the priests (usually three) on the south side of the chancel of a church

SHAFT-RING: 12th- and 13th-centuries feature consisting of a ring round a circular pier or a shaft attached to a pier

SOFFIT: Underside of an arch, lintel etc.

SLYPE: A passage, usually in the form of a tunnel, leading from the Cloisters to the precinct. The Eastern Slype led to the Monks' cemetery

SPANDREL: Triangular surface between two arches

SPLAY: Chamfer, usually of the jamb of a window

STALL: Carved seat made of wood or stone

STIFF-LEAF: E.E. type of foliage of many-lobed shapes

STOUP: Vessel for holding holy water, usually placed near a door

STRING COURSE: Projecting horizontal band or moulding set in the surface of a wall

TIERCERON: *see* Vault

TRACERY: Ribwork in the upper part of a window, or used decoratively in blank arches or vaults

TRANSEPT: Transverse part of a cross-shaped church

TREFOIL, QUATREFOIL, or CINQUEFOIL: Three, four or five lobes or leaf shapes in Gothic tracery

TRIBUNE: *see* Gallery

TRIFORIUM, TRIFORIA: Arcaded wall passage or blank arcading facing the nave at the height of the aisle roof and below the clerestory (q.v.) windows (see gallery)

TYMPANUM: Space between the lintel of a doorway and the arch above it

VAULT: Barrel Vault, tunnel vault: vault of semicircular section

Groin vault: identical shapes intersecting each other, as in the Worcester crypt

Lierne: tertiary rib, that is a rib which does not spring either from one of the main springers or from the central boss (see figs. 85, 87 and 88)

Ribbed vault: vault with ribs added to the groins (see fig. 61)

Ridge rib: rib along the longitudinal or transverse ridge of the vault — early 13th century

Tierceron: secondary rib, a rib which issues from the springing of the vault or the central boss and leads to place on the ridge rib (see vault with extra ribs springing from the corners of the bays fig. 70)

VOUSSOIR: Wedge-shaped stone used in arch construction

WATERLEAF: Leaf shape used in later 12th-century capitals

BIBLIOGRAPHY

There is a dearth of accessible publications on the architecture, sculpture, painting and stained glass of the cathedral and it is hoped that this book will be the first of a series which will cover every aspect of the cathedral's development.

The most important sources for this book have been the papers by the Rev Robert Willis, dating from the mid-19th century but even now only superseded in detail; the entry for the cathedral in Pevsner's *Worcestershire*, and the papers resulting from the visit of the British Archaeological Association in 1975.

Baker, N. *et al.* From Roman to Medieval Worcester: development and planning in the Anglo-Saxon City, *Antiquity*, Vol. 66, No. 250, March 1992, pp. 65-74

Barker, P.A. ed *The Origins of Worcester; Trans. Worcs. Archaeol. Soc.* 3rd series, Vol. 2 1968-69 Worcester 1970, (particularly pp. 27-34)

Barker, P.A., Cubberley, A.L., Crowfoot, E. and Radford, C.A.R. Two burials under the Refectory at Worcester Cathedral, *Med.Archaeol.* 18 (1974), 146-151

Bassett, S. Churches in Worcester before and after the conversion of the Anglo-Saxons, *The Antiquaries Journal*, Vol. LXIX, Part II, 1989, pp. 225-256

Carver, M.O.H. ed. *Medieval Worcester: An Archaeological Framework; Trans. Worcs. Archaeol. Soc.* 3rd series, Vol. 7 1980. (particularly pp. 31ff, 115ff, 127ff, 139ff, 143ff, and 298-300.)

Craze, M. *Lectures on Worcester Cathedral*, Worcester 1988

Guy, C. Excavations at Worcester Cathedral, 1981-1991, *Trans. Worcs. Archaeol. Soc.* 1994, 3rd Series, Vol. 14, pp. 1-73

Henry, Avril, ed. *The Eton Roundels, Eton College*, Ms 177, Scolar Press, 1991

Heslop, T.A., 'Worcester Cathedral Chapterhouse and the Harmony of the Testaments', in Binski, P. & Noel, W. (eds.), *New Offerings, Ancient Treasures; Studies in Medieval Art for George Henderson,* Stroud 2001, pp. 280-311

Lubin, H. *The Worcester Pilgrim*, Worcester, 1990. Describes the discovery of a well-preserved pilgrim burial in the crossing of the cathedral, and discusses its implications.

Medieval Art and Architecture at Worcester Cathedral, British Archaeological Association Transactions for the year 1975, London, 1978. Includes an extensive bibliography relating to the cathedral.

Pevsner, N. *The Buildings of England: Worcestershire*, Penguin, 1968, pp. 293-314

Robson, S. Report on the Water Gate Excavations, Worcester Cathedral, 1993, *Trans. Worcs. Archaeol. Soc.*, 3rd Series, Vol. 16, 1998

Willis Bund, J.W. *The Civil War in Worcestershire 1643-1646*, and *The Scotch Invasion of 1651*, Birmingham 1905

Worcester Cathedral Notes and Monographs 1909-1914, Cathedral Library. A miscellany of important papers relating to the architecture and sculpture of the cathedral

Wild, C. A*n illustration of the Architecture and Sculpture of the Cathedral Church of Worcester*, London, 1823

Willis, R. The Architectural History of the Cathedral and Monastery at Worcester, *Archaeol. Journ.*, XX (1863), pp. 83, 254, 301

Willis, R. The Crypt and the Chapter House of Worcester Cathedral, *RIBA Journal XIII* (1862/63), p. 213

Willis, R. Notes on the Norman Work in the Chapter House of Worcester Cathedral, *Archaeol. Journ.*, XX (1863), p. 17

The Reports of the Annual Symposia on the Archaeology of the Cathedral at Worcester, 1991 onwards. Worcester Chapter Office

Index

Page numbers in italics relate to illustrations. Saints are indexed under their given name.
Churches are indexed under St.